FULL METAL PANIC!™

Fighting Boy Meets Girl

Volume 1
Story by Shouji Gatou
Art by Shikidouji

D0973193

POP FICTION

A **TOKYOPOP** Prose Novel

TOKYOPOP Inc.
5900 Wilshire Boulevard, Suite 2000
Los Angeles, CA 90036
www.TOKYOPOP.com

Story	Shouji Gatou
Illustrations	Shikidouji
Translation	Duane Johnson
English Adaptation	Ben Arntz
Design and Layout	James Lee & Courtney H. Geter
Cover Design	James Lee & Yoseph Middleton
Creative Director	Ann Marie Horne
Senior Editor	Jenna Winterberg
Editor	Kara Allison Stambach
Digital Managing Editor	Chris Buford
Production Manager	Liz Brizzi
Managing Editor	Vy Nguyen
Editor-in-Chief	Rob Tokar
VP of Production	Ron Klamert
Publisher	Mike Kiley
President and COO	John Parker
CEO & Chief Creative Officer	Stuart Levy

ISBN: 978-1-4278-0243-9

First TOKYOPOP printing: September 2007
10 9 8 7 6 5 4 3 2
Printed in the USA

FULL METAL PANIC! TATAKAU BOY MEETS GIRL
© 1998 Shouji Gatou, Shikidouji
First published in Japan in 1998
by FUJIMISHOBO CO., LTD., Tokyo.
English translation rights arranged with KADOKAWA SHOTEN PUBLISHING CO.,
LTD., Tokyo through TUTTLE-MORI AGENCY, INC., Tokyo.

English text copyright © 2007 TOKYOPOP Inc.

FULL METAL PANIC!™

CONTENTS

011 Prologue

019 Ch.1 School Assignment

079 Ch.2 Underwater Scene

123 Ch.3 Bad Trip

183 Ch.4 Field of Giants

231 Ch.5 Black Technology

297 Epilogue

305 Afterword

PEEPING TOM, STRAY CHILD, OR STALKER? FOR BEAUTIFUL KANAME AND TRANSFER STUDENT SOUSUKE, THIS IS ONLY THE BEGINNING.

A spiral of nonsensical letters appears. As Kaname stares, a hidden seal within her breaks.

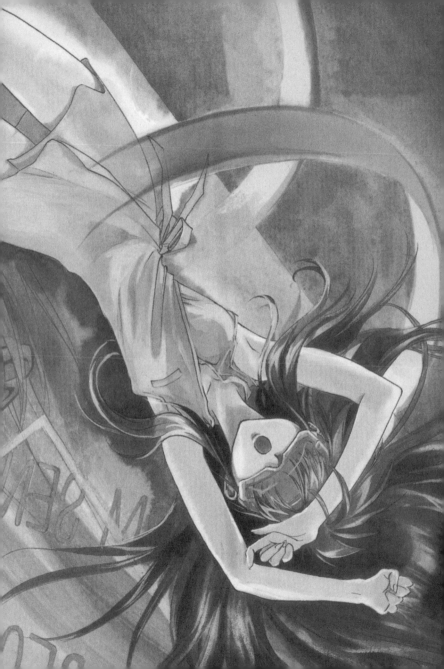

KANAME LOWERS HER GUN. SHE SLOWLY REACHES OUT AND HUGS SOUSUKE.

"SAGARA, LET'S GO HOME TOGETHER . . ."

AS. A•S. 1 <ABBR.> ANGLO-SAXON.

AS. A•S. 2 <ABBR.> [MILITARY] ARM SLAVE.

ARM SLAVE ['ärm "slAv] [MILITARY]

<FROM ARMORED MOBILE MASTER-SLAVE SYSTEM>

MECHANIZED ASSAULT TROOPER, AS.

—KENKYUSHA'S NEW ENGLISH-JAPANESE DICTIONARY,

FIFTH EDITION

ARM SLAVE, USUALLY 26' OR MORE IN HEIGHT, AN ARMED

AND ARMORED ATTACK WEAPON PATTERNED AFTER THE HUMAN

BODY. DEVELOPED DURING THE LATE 1980S. MECHANIZED ASSAULT

TROOPER. AS.

—IWANAMI SHOTEN KOUJIEN, FOURTH EDITION

Prologue

"Pay attention, Sousuke!"

In contrast to the after-school ruckus, Kaname Chidori spoke decidedly seriously. A strong-willed girl, her black hair reached her hips and was held in place by a neat red ribbon. She conducted her instructions to the male student in front of her with a rigid index finger.

"We need two-thousand sheets of letter-sized copy paper. It's in bundles of five-hundred sheets, so just sneak in and get four of those. Got it?"

"Understood." Sousuke Sagara responded crisply.

There was little about Sousuke that wasn't crisp—his words, his collar, and his movements all were rigid. His face was tense and unforgiving.

He glanced at the door to the staff room.

"You know where to find the paper, right?"

"Yes. It's all the way in the back, next to the copier."

"Good. Let's review the plan."

"You'll create a diversion, engaging Mister Sayama in conversation. While you have his attention, I'll plunder the paper and make a speedy withdrawal."

Satisfied, Kaname nodded.

"I wouldn't call it 'plundering,' exactly. After all, it isn't our fault there was a staff miscommunication that led to a misprint on the Drawing Club's flyers! We're not plundering, we're just covering the losses."

Deciding not to object to this justification, Sousuke focused on another concern. "What if your diversion doesn't provide sufficient cover? The teacher might notice."

"It's your job to scheme, finding a way to get in and out unseen."

"Very well, I will *scheme*."

"Okay, Sousuke, let's go."

Kaname led the way inside. She made her way toward the rear of the office, greeting all the teachers she knew along the way. Eventually, she reached the overused copier in the back.

Next to the nearly obsolete machine, a forty-year-old social studies teacher sat grading tests. Kaname positioned herself between the man and the machine, hoping it was enough to keep him from spotting Sousuke.

"Hello, Mister Sayama!"

Mister Sayama's chair creaked as he swiveled to greet her. "Miss Chidori. What brings you here today?"

"Well, I have a question that I forgot to ask yesterday."

"When we were talking about ancient India?"

"Yes. I have to know—in ancient India, did everybody have names as weird as Chandragupta II?"

Mister Sayama laughed heartily. "That's a strange question! But the name has a particular meaning. You see, the Gupta Empire—"

POP!

Following the firecracker-like noise, thick white smoke spread through the air behind Kaname.

"What the—"

By the time Kaname turned around to see what had happened, she couldn't see two inches in front of her face.

"What's happening?" demanded Sayama, coughing violently.

The smoke began to spread through the staff room. One of the other teachers in the office screamed, then another. Soon, everyone was in a complete state of panic.

"What *is* this?" Choking violently, Kaname steadied herself on a nearby bookshelf. Someone firmly grabbed her arm.

"Sousuke?"

"Mission accomplished. Speedy withdrawal."

"Oh . . ."

With the bundles of paper under one arm and Kaname's wrist in the other, Sousuke emerged from the smoke; then, he made a break for the exit.

"Save us! It's a fire!" yelled one teacher.

The ceiling sprinklers activated, drenching the room.

"Save us! It's a flood!" hollered another teacher.

Pushing through the cacophony, Sousuke and Kaname rushed out of the staff office and continued running until they were safely in a far-off hallway.

Kaname caught her breath.

"We should be safe here," assessed Sousuke.

They both were soaked from head to toe thanks to the sprinklers' good intentions.

Looking slightly less than amused, Kaname wrung the water from her skirt.

"What on Earth was that?"

"It was a smoke bomb," Sousuke answered matter-of-factly.

"*What?*"

"You said to scheme. The smoke bomb cut all the visibility in the office, so we could get the paper out safely without them seeing our faces. It's much more effective than a crude diversion. To avert suspicion, I'll make a phone call later as either the IRA or the JRA or some other terrorist organization claiming responsibility. That way—"

Whock!

Kaname delivered a right hook that sent Sousuke spinning to the floor. For about three seconds, he remained motionless. Then, he rose quickly to his feet.

"That hurt."

"Shut up! You . . . you maniac war nut! What's the big idea? Look—you ruined the paper!"

Kaname shoved the sopping bundles of paper in his face.

"Perhaps we still could use it after we dry it."

"You are such a moron! I don't care if you are some kind of secret mercenary—you need to learn some common sense!"

Sousuke grew quiet and began to sweat. He looked like a cat that had been scolded for bringing home a gift of a decapitated mouse—he had been trying to help, in his own way.

For Kaname, Sousuke's good intentions made it that much harder to chastise him.

Oh, good grief, she thought, bringing her hands to her head.

After all, it wasn't Sousuke's fault that he grew up in international hot zones and had no idea how to live in peaceful Japan.

Consequently, no matter how hard he tried, everything he did seemed to backfire, creating trouble where none existed previously. Pretty much everyone at school thought he was an idiot of the highest degree.

Jeez. What did I ever do to deserve someone this useless? Kaname lamented internally.

But Kaname already knew the answer. If she didn't, she would have stopped being his friend a long time ago. Kaname had an obligation to get into Sousuke's business, to lecture him, and to deal with the aftermath of his messes. There was a reason she could not hate him.

She suddenly remembered the various complex reasons Sousuke was the way he was.

She knew Sousuke had another identity, one that he kept secret from the rest of the students, who thought he was nothing more than a useless war nut.

Outside the walls of the high school, Sousuke Sagara also was secretly a first-class soldier, part of a top-notch military organization.

Kaname knew this because of a certain incident.

It was through this incident that Kaname and Sousuke had become acquainted. Kaname recalled the circumstances behind their meeting: There had been grave danger, blossoming feelings, and a huge mystery—one that remained partially unsolved.

That event's aftereffects still lingered in their everyday lives.

Indeed, it all started one month earlier. . . .

CHAPTER 1
School Assignment

April 15, 21:37 (Local Time)
Eastern Soviet Union
50 Miles Southeast of Khabarovsk

I'd just as soon die.

Violently bouncing around in an automobile's interior, the girl continued to make grim assessments of her situation.

Mud from the sloshy road splattered across the windshield, obscuring the coniferous trees that barely were visible in the farthest reaches of the headlights.

The girl caught a glimpse of her reflection in the side-view mirror: a pale face, gnawing on her thumb as if possessed.

I should be tanner from tennis practice. Why am I so pallid?

How long has it been since my last tennis practice? A week? A month?

A year?

Time's not important. I can't go home, anyway.

It'd be easiest if they just killed me now.

"Almost there," shouted the vehicle's driver, a gruff man who was wearing a stiff military uniform. "In just a couple of miles, we'll be in the mountain district. From there, you'll be able to return to Japan."

Liar. We'll never get away in a vehicle like this.

Those people will capture me, drug me, strip me, and lock me up again in that water tank—that deep, dark water tank, a place where nothing exists but endless, meaningless questions. No matter how much I beg, they won't let me out.

"I'll do anything, just let me out!"

They won't hear me. I can't even hear myself.

Gradually, they will break me.

The only thing I have left is biting my nails. That's all I can do. It is my only joy. Nails are fantastic: They hurt, they bleed. They're great. Blood comes out, it dissolves. Nails . . . nails . . . naillllls.

"Stop that!" the man brushed the girl's hand away from her mouth.

For a moment, she stared absently at him. "Let me bite—or else, kill me. Let me b-bi-bite."

The man's face contorted with pity as the girl's speech devolved into a pathetic stutter, like that of a broken tape deck. His sympathy turned to anger.

"Those scum bags did some bad things to you, didn't they?"

A bright flash of light behind the vehicle punctuated the man's sentiment, inspiring him to crank the wheel furiously. The light painted a streak across the sky as it sailed over the fleeing Jeep.

A rocket!

An explosion sent flames and debris hurtling toward the front of the Jeep, which skidded sideways. The windshield shattered, and the jeep toppled and rolled through the flames.

Not wearing a seat belt, the girl was tossed clear of the wreck through the side window.

If she had taken a breath at that moment, or if she had opened her mouth to scream, the whirling flames would have scorched her lungs. Sadly, she lacked the willpower to scream.

Crashing shoulder first into the snowy, muddy ground, she tumbled to a stop. Although laid out like a doll, the girl had no desire to move.

But her cloudy consciousness cleared. When she slowly lifted her head, she saw the mostly destroyed Jeep snapped in half like a twig, its rear wheels spinning futilely.

The girl tried to get up, but there was no strength in her shoulder—it was either broken or dislocated. Oddly enough, however, she felt no pain. She half-crawled toward the automobile wreckage, spotting the battered and bloody driver pinned beneath some of the car's plating.

"Take this," he gasped, holding out a CD case with a trembling hand. "Go . . . south . . ."

His eyes were wet with tears.

"Hurry. Run."

And that was it for him. His tear-filled eyes were still half-open, forever frozen in anguish.

The girl did not understand why the man was crying. Pain? Fear of death? Something else?

Suddenly, her survival instincts kicked in. She stood, took the CD case, and began to plop one dirty, bloody foot after another through the mud. She had no idea which way south was, but she walked in a straight line regardless, continually biting her thumbnail as she went.

Rotors chopped noisily through the air. An engine howled as it sucked in air and gas. It was a helicopter—and it was approaching quickly! The forest swayed in the man-made wind.

The girl looked up to see a gray attack helicopter, its body rugged and gnarled like an old tree.

How ugly, she thought.

"Halt!" warned the helicopter's external speaker. "Or you will be shot to death!"

Of course, she did not halt. She continued to drudge in a straight line.

"Where do you think you're going?" The helicopter's machine gun fired a few rounds into the ground near the girl. Chunks of earth flew through the air, and the girl fell to the ground.

"Bad girls get punished."

As she tried to pick herself up using her one good arm, a smattering of shots struck the ground around her.

The impact of the bullets in the ground near the girl made it impossible for her to get up. The sound of laughter came through the helicopter's loudspeaker.

Determined, the girl continued to crawl.

"Oh, poor little girl. Look how worn out she is! And still, she keeps—" the voice cut out, leaving only the sound of the chopper's spinning blades.

"Look out! It's an AS. Increase alti—"

The high-pitched sound of crushing metal interrupted the pilot. The helicopter became a veritable spark factory. The girl looked up and saw something sticking out of the machine's nose.

A knife?

It was a huge knife—a throwing knife as large as a person. The red-hot blade stuck clear through the helicopter's nose.

Fighting a losing battle with gravity, the attack helicopter lurched in a great spin. Fishtailing like crazy, it hurtled toward the girl. She had neither the time nor the aspiration to move from its path. She stayed rooted in place, watching the hunk of iron that would bring her demise.

Then, out of the corner of her eye, she caught a glimpse of an extremely large figure.

The mysterious figure straddled her, spread its arms, braced its legs, and stood in front of the oncoming helicopter.

Crash!

Scraps of metal flew around, and small parts rained from the sky. The grating sounds of grinding gears and uselessly spinning turbines played an aircraft's dirge duet.

When the girl looked up, she saw that the giant humanlike shape had caught the helicopter with its upper body. Its back bent vigorously, and steam gushed from the joints in its arms, shoulders, hips, and knees.

It began to walk, its heavy footsteps kicking up chunks of dirt and snow. The machine carried the helicopter a sufficient distance from the girl, whereupon it tossed the whirlybird into the forest. The chopper wreckage fell to the ground and exploded.

The machine, which was roughly twenty-six feet tall, turned around. It was backlit by the flaming helicopter.

Finally, the girl was able to get a good look at the mysterious behemoth, which greatly resembled an athletic person with its long legs, tight waist, massive chest, and burly arms; it just happened to be coated with armor plating. The machine looked like a fighter pilot wearing a helmet, and it carried a proportional gun and backpack, just like a person would.

"It's an . . . Arm Slave, an assault trooper!"

The AS, a mechanized giant, returned to her side.

"Are you injured?" asked the humanoid machine in a calm male voice. "I had to use an anti-tank dagger because the helicopter was so close to you. My shot cannon would have been much too powerful."

Still in a state of shock, the girl said nothing. The AS knelt, braced itself with one of its giant mechanical hands, and lowered its head. It looked like a scene from a fairy tale: a gray giant kneeling before a tattered princess.

Sssssss.

A hatch on the Arm Slave's torso opened, and a soldier popped up through the hatch behind the machine's head.

He wore a black pilot suit and small, lightweight headgear that made him appear vaguely like a ninja when the light silhouetted him.

First-aid kit in hand, the AS operator climbed out of the weapon.

He was young and Asian, with messy black hair, sharp eyes, a knitted brow, and a tight-lipped mouth.

The soldier was still a boy—probably not much older than the girl he had come to rescue. But there was nothing childlike about his demeanor; he left no impression of the innocence and irresponsibility characteristic of boys his age.

"Where are you hurt?" asked the pilot. He spoke in Japanese, which surprised the girl.

When she didn't respond, he asked her if she understood Japanese. She nodded almost imperceptibly.

"Are you with that man?" she asked, pointing to the spot where the driver lay dead.

"Yes. I'm also part of Mithril."

"Mithril?"

"An undercover military organization with no national affiliation."

Again, the girl did not know how to respond.

As the soldier began to administer first aid, the girl suddenly became cognizant of her intense pain. Her breathing became ragged, but she managed to speak through the wheezing.

"He died."

"Yes, it appears he did."

"He was trying to set me free."

"That's the kind of man he was."

"Doesn't it make you sad?"

The young soldier temporarily stopped wrapping her shoulder in tape so he could consider his emotional state. "I'm not sure," he finally said.

After he finished wrapping the girl's shoulder and arm, the young man began to prod and poke the girl's body without restraint or bashfulness.

"What are you going to do with me?"

"First, I'll take you in my AS to the transport helicopter's LZ. Once we're on the helicopter, we'll return to the mother ship, which is at sea. I don't know what happens after that—that's where our duty ends."

"*Our* duty?"

As if answering her question, two more Arm Slaves appeared, clearing a path through the trees while keeping a vigilant watch on the surroundings.

They looked almost identical to the first one, and they carried rifles and missile launchers.

"Don't worry: They're with me."

The pain began to take an even greater toll on the girl—her field of vision narrowed, and her thoughts grew cloudy. She couldn't remember where she was.

"What's your name?" she squeaked.

"It's best if you don't talk. You'll waste your strength."

"Please, tell me."

Hesitantly, the soldier contemplated revealing himself.

"Sagara. Sousuke Sagara."

Before he even finished saying it, however, the girl had passed out.

April 15, 16:11 (Greenwich Mean Time)
Sea of Japan, Depth: 330 Feet
Amphibious Assault Submarine Tuatha de Danaan

Armed with a clipboard and a fruit-flavored Calorie Mate, Sousuke entered the giant submarine's overly spacious hangar to work on his post-mission report.

Most of the ship's weaponry—Arm Slaves, transport helicopters, VTOL fighters, and the like—were lined up there. Sousuke gazed at one that was being repaired.

"Hey, Sousuke!" called an overbearing voice.

Sousuke turned around to see his colleague, Sergeant Kurz Weber.

Blond-haired and blue-eyed with a small chin and big eyes, Kurz was movie-star handsome. His long, perfectly styled hair added a touch of genderless charm. When he smiled, women's hearts beat faster.

As soon as he opened his mouth, however . . .

"Why the long face? Constipated? Hemorrhoids?"

No dignity. No class.

"I'm in perfect health," Sousuke responded absentmindedly, taking a bite of his Calorie Mate.

"You're really dense, you know that?" Kurz's gaze wandered to the AS that was being repaired. Its armor was off already. "Wow, they already cracked it open, huh?"

"Apparently, they're conducting a detailed inspection of the frame system."

"Well, you were pretty hard on it. I mean, you caught a helicopter! Weren't you scared?"

"No. It wasn't an activity beyond the specs of the M9."

The model AS both Sousuke and Kurz used was called a M9 Gernsback. It was totally cutting edge—not yet widely used in military circles. Compared to previous models of Arm Slaves, the M9 had extraordinary power and agility.

"I guess, but the M9 is the only mech that could pull that stunt," decided Kurz as he took a seat on an empty ammo case. He stared at the line of M9s in the hangar.

The Arm Slave was born in the mid-1980s. At the time, U.S. President Ronald Reagan strongly supported the development of a robot force to go along with the Star Wars strategic defense project:

"The next great development in localized dispute resolution."

"A grand technical challenge!"

"A labor-saving contribution to infantry forces!"

Driven by suspicious rhetoric, the AS became reality just three years later. The humanoid weapon once thought to be an impossible joke now ran at speeds of more than sixty miles per hour, employed numerous weapons, and matched a tank in terms of strength.

Specialists were blown away—after all, non-military bipedal robots barely could take a step or two without falling over.

What genius had masterminded this project? What think tank had developed it?

"It's technology from interplanetary visitors!" claimed UFO fanatics, temporarily boosting the sales of their magazines and books.

Eventually, however, people came to regard the AS the same way they saw the cruise missile or stealth fighter jet—as a very high-tech weapon.

About ten years later, AS technology continued to make explosive progress. It got to the point where it was dangerous to approach one carelessly, even in an attack helicopter.

A thought interrupted Kurz's stare. "Hey, Sousuke, about that girl you picked up . . ."

"Will she live?"

"Yeah, but she was pretty doped up."

"Narcotics?"

"Cannabinoids or something like that—they still don't know exactly, but they think it came from the KGB research facility. I don't know what kind of experiments they're doing there, but they're pretty damn cruel."

"Will she recover?"

"Who knows? Even if she does, it probably will take a long time."

Sousuke didn't know what to say. Although the superior officers seemed to know what kind of guinea pig the girl was, they didn't share that information with Sousuke and Kurz. It was protocol, really: Frontline combatants rarely had all the details.

The man who died in the Jeep was a spy from Mithril's intelligence bureau. Saving the girl wasn't part of his original mission, which was to dig up information on the KGB research facility. However, he had suffered a tremendous twinge of conscience and put his own life at risk to rescue the test subject.

In spite of the spy's death, the CD with the top-secret information still made it back into Mithril's hands, thanks to Sousuke and the others.

Breaking the silence, Master Sergeant Melissa Mao quickly entered the hangar. "There you are."

Solidly in her mid-twenties, Mao was an American of Chinese descent. Her short black hair nicely framed her pretty face without masking her true, spirited nature. Like Sousuke and Kurz, Mao was a skilled AS operator. The three of them often were lumped together as a team, and Mao always was the leader.

"Good work on the overtime," said Mao.

Sousuke grunted and nodded.

"What's up, girl?" said Kurz.

"Wipe that grin off your face, Mister. You always look like the comic relief around here."

"Do you know who you're talking to? It's *me*, Kurz Weber, model extraordinaire. This delicious face graced the pages of *Esquire*, you know."

"Oh yeah, I think I saw that. Wasn't it a farce—like that Charlie Sheen movie *Hot Shots?*"

"You bitch."

Quickly, like a cat, Mao reached out and grabbed Kurz's cheek. He yelped.

"What did you call me?" she demanded.

"Jus' the smar'es, preddies', mos' debendable—"

"That's what I thought," she said, letting go of his face.

Quietly nibbling, Sousuke watched the whole exchange.

Mao noticed when he swallowed.

"Those things any good?"

Smiling, he nodded. "Just the right sweetness."

"Cool. Sousuke, the lieutenant commander wants to see you."

"Understood."

"You too, playboy."

"Aw, man! I thought you said we were off duty!"

"Consider this a countermand," said Mao, laughing. "I, however, *am* off duty. If you need me, I'll be in the bath." She cackled as she left.

"If that bitch knew what was good for her," commented Kurz, "she'd be clawing her name into my back."

As she walked away, Kurz flipped her backside the bird.

"What kind of curse is that?" wondered Sousuke.

Knock knock!

"Come in!"

Sousuke and Kurz filed into the small room filled with documents, bookshelves, and a large man clad in an olive-green combat uniform—Lieutenant Commander Kalinin. Although Kalinin had long gray hair, his beard and mustache were cropped short.

"Reporting as ordered, sir," stated Sousuke, crisply saluting.

"Yeah, here we are." Kurz submitted a halfhearted salute.

Indifferent to Kurz's attitude, Lieutenant Commander Kalinin looked up from the documents he was reading.

"There's a mission." Lieutenant Commander Kalinin didn't beat around the bush. He tossed a file folder toward Sousuke and Kurz. "Take a look at this."

"Yes, sir," replied Sousuke.

"You got it," quipped Kurz.

The documents in the file appeared to be a personal history, including a black-and-white photo of a smiling Asian girl. Roughly age twelve in the photo, the girl was nestled up against a woman, ostensibly her mother. With fair skin and clear-cut features, she was a lovely child.

Kurz whistled. "I'll bet she grows up to be hot."

"Actually, the photo is four years old," announced the lieutenant commander. "She's sixteen, now."

"So, where's the picture of her now?"

"We don't have one."

As he already was accustomed to Kurz's manner, Sousuke paid him no attention, focusing instead on reading the girl's biographical information.

According to the brief, her name was Kaname Chidori, and she lived in Tokyo, Japan. Kaname was a student in one of Tokyo's many high schools. Her father was a U.N. High Commissioner. She had one sibling: an eleven-year-old sister who lived with her father in New York City. Her mother had died three years earlier.

There was additional information: height, blood type, medical history, and more—the report spared no detail.

One sentence popped out at Sousuke: *Probability of being a W*******d: 88% (according to Miller Statistics Act).*

Sousuke knew that the word that had been censored haphazardly with black marker was the real reason Kurz and he were being assigned the mission.

"So, what happened to her?" asked Kurz.

"Nothing," responded Kalinin. "Yet."

"Huh?" Kurz grunted his confusion.

Turning slightly in his creaky chair, the lieutenant commander looked at a map of the world that was mounted on the wall. It was up to date with the latest national borders—the complexly divided Soviet bloc, the split of the northern and southern Chinese territories, and the scribble of lines that made up the Middle East.

"All you two need to know is that there are a number of enemy agencies, including the KGB, that might want to kidnap Kaname Chidori."

"Why?" inquired Kurz.

"That," Kalinin said stoutly, "is something you gentlemen do not need to know."

"Oh, right."

It all seemed pretty vague to Kurz. This girl, Kaname Chidori, was only a *potential* target.

"What, exactly, is our mission?" pressed Sousuke.

"You'll guard the girl, naturally. I'm giving this one to you guys because you're both fluent in Japanese."

"I guess that makes sense."

Kurz's father was a newspaper correspondent and, consequently, Kurz had lived in the Edogawa section of Tokyo until he was fourteen. Thus, he spoke the language like a pro.

"I've briefed Master Sergeant Mao already. The three of you will handle this."

That seemed like an awful lot of work to Kurz. "Whoa, just the three of us?"

"I barely can spare that many. It's decided already."

"Rough," assessed Kurz.

"That's why you're here."

Sousuke, Kurz, and Mao were more than just AS pilots, they were highly trained soldiers capable of airborne landings, reconnaissance, combat, and more. They were members of a team picked from numerous candidates. And to them, an AS was just one of the many tools of their trade.

"Upon Mao's insistence, I've granted you Class B equipment."

The two soldiers' jaws dropped open.

"We're taking an Arm Slave?" asked Sousuke.

"Yes."

"But it's in the heart of a major city!" protested Kurz.

"You'll just have to operate in ECS invisible mode," reasoned Kalinin.

Though the technology was pioneered for Arm Slaves, many modern weapons used some form of ECS—or Electromagnetic Camouflage System. Using hologram technology, the cutting-edge stealth equipment could hide very large objects from radar and infrared rays. Mithril's ECS systems were so advanced that they could nullify visible light wavelengths.

In other words, it made them invisible.

It took a lot of energy, so invisibility was not practical (or even possible) during combat, but it was no problem when the vehicle was sitting still or hiding.

"You'll take one M9 with you. Armament will be minimal, so carry two external condenser packs."

"Check," affirmed Kurz.

"It's imperative that this mission is kept top secret."

"Say what?" Kurz frowned.

"If the Japanese government finds out," Kalinin continued, "it'll get messy. So you must protect Kaname without her or anyone else knowing. But you still must be ready when trouble comes."

"That sounds very . . ." Kurz struggled for words.

"Difficult," concluded Sousuke. Guarding someone without her knowledge or permission was beyond absurd.

"Depending on how you operate, it shouldn't be that difficult. This girl—Kaname Chidori—spends most of her time at a co-ed public high school. Our youngest soldier is the same age as she is, and he's even Japanese."

"Oh, ho ho!" Kurz lit up and turned to Sousuke, who blinked a few times under the scrutiny.

"You don't mean—"

"We're forging the student transfer papers right now."

And Kalinin signed the directive.

April 16, 11:50 (Greenwich Mean Time)
Off the Coast of the Tsugaru Peninsula, Depth: 330 Feet
Tuatha de Danaan Briefing Room #1

"Say 'cheese,' Sousuke."

Sousuke scowled at the camera and at Kurz, its operator.

"Come on, man," goaded Kurz. "Don't you want a nice picture on your student ID?"

Calling on little-used muscles, Sousuke formed an expression that looked more like a facial neuralgia than a smile.

"Close enough." Kurz snapped the picture.

Like an elastic band that is stretched and released, Sousuke's face instantly returned to its most comfortable, sullen expression.

Kurz sighed.

April 17, 21:20 (Greenwich Mean Time)
Off the Coast of Kinkazan Island, Depth: 260 Feet
Tuatha de Danaan Mess Hall

"What is all this?" Sousuke asked, staring at the collection of items strewn across the table. He picked up some of the objects and scowled at them: a brush, some hair gel, a portable CD player, CDs by Hiroshi Itsuki and SMAP, assorted charms from Narita-san temple, a Game Boy, a Mister Junko watch, cigarettes, energy drinks, glossy magazines, and a few other miscellaneous items of that nature.

Melissa Mao beamed. "I went around the ship and gathered up all the things a typical Japanese high school student might have."

"I see." Somewhat confused, Sousuke picked up a little square of vinyl that contained a rubbery-looking circle.

"That's a condom," said Mao.

"I know. But I can't figure out why a high school boy would need one."

43

"Don't play innocent, you hornball!"

"As a matter of fact, I have used them many times," said Sousuke. "They can hold an entire liter of liquid."

Melissa Mao's mouth dropped open.

"Yes, if you've lost your canteen in the jungle, these can be a real lifesaver," Sousuke concluded earnestly.

"Is that so?" Master Sergeant Mao rolled her eyes.

April 18, 10:06 (Greenwich Mean Time)
Off the Coast of the Boso Peninsula, Depth: 165 Feet
Tuatha de Danaan Briefing Room #1

Clutching a remote, Kurz ushered Sousuke in front of an LCD screen. "Okay, take a look at this. These are Japanese high school students, so pay attention."

When Kurz hit play, a generic-looking classroom filled the screen. It looked like it was evening, and there were only two students in the classroom. Despite there being plenty of space in the room, they were standing in the corner, very close to each other.

"I've always thought of you as a childhood friend," admitted the young man, slowly letting out the words, "until now. I can't believe it took me this long to realize the way I feel about you."

"Oh, Tohru!" gasped the girl, hugging the boy.

As the young man leaned in to kiss her, the door to the classroom creaked open. Turning in surprise, the couple in the corner saw another student standing in the doorway.

"Naomi!" called Tohru.

"How could you?" demanded Naomi, who ran away in tears.

The boy started to chase after her, but the girl in the corner pulled on his sleeve and told him to let her go.

Kurz hit the pause button.

"Why did she run?" asked Sousuke. "Isn't the girl in the corner her enemy?"

Kurz blinked in awe of Sousuke's lack of social sense.

"Unless . . . Naomi now knows a secret that could get her eliminated. She ran because she's a survivor. Clever girl!"

"Or something like that," said Kurz, rolling his eyes.

45

April 19, 03:30 (Japan Standard Time)
Off the Coast of the Miura Peninsula
Tuatha de Danaan Flight Deck

As the Tuatha de Danaan rested half-submerged in the sea like a vigilant hippo, the hatch to its flight deck groaned open, revealing the tarmac from which the Arm Slaves, combat choppers, and VTOL planes could take off.

A seven-rotor transport helicopter sat on the flight deck, waiting for permission to leave. The cargo hold was stocked full of all kinds of gear, including an Arm Slave M9.

After tossing his small bag behind his seat, Sousuke fastened his seat belt. He checked to make sure he hadn't forgotten anything vital, such as the forged student ID that was stashed in his breast pocket.

Mao, who sat next to him, stared at the ID card.

"You put your real name on there?"

"I did. But I don't exist in Japanese record books, anyway, so if a problem arises, I always could change my name."

"Oh, okay."

"It's not a problem. Let's get a move on."

The helicopter began to prepare for takeoff.

"Are you nervous? I mean, it's your first day of school," pointed out Kurz from his position in the back seat.

"I'll do my best," replied Sousuke.

"Tessa seemed worried," commented Mao, referring to the submarine's captain.

"I'm not surprised. It's an important mission," said Sousuke, eliciting a simultaneous sigh from both Mao and Kurz.

Before they could continue the conversation, the pilot of the helicopter informed them that it was time to take off.

April 20, 08:20 (Japan Standard Time)
Suburbs of Tokyo, Japan
A Road 350 Feet North of Jindai Municipal High School

"Totally sucked," said a disgruntled Kaname Chidori.

Her dark brown eyes wandered for a moment, surveying the group of students walking with her. As Kaname walked, the black hair that hung clear to her hips swayed to and fro at a leisurely pace that was in great contrast to her walking speed.

"Completely and totally sucked," she concluded after a moment of thought.

Kyouko Tokiwa, a classmate, said "Gee, Kana, you haven't talked about anything else all morning. Was it really that terrible?"

"Worse!" insisted Kaname. "He talked incessantly without ever actually *saying* anything. I did him the favor of going out with him and everything, so you'd think he could find at least one interesting thing to talk about."

Like you? thought Kyouko. *His father's a designer, he's got a friend in the J-league—seems interesting to me.* To avoid trouble, though, she just said "Uh-huh."

"I mean, there's the life of Zhuge Liang, the pollution in the Pacific, religious strife in the Middle East—"

"Uh-huh."

"Are you even listening to me, Kyouko? Or are you just saying 'uh-huh'?"

"Uh-huh."

"Stop that, Kyouko! The least you can do is listen to my post-date recap. After all, you're the one who introduced him to me."

"He asked me to."

"If someone asked you to sell me off to Macao, would you do that, too?"

"Uh-huh!"

"Ha ha! You brat," Kaname said fondly.

As the school came into view, they could see a line of students extending from the front door.

"Oh man, security searches," groaned Kaname, the victim of many random bag and pocket searches.

"Yeah, it sure is. You don't have anything illegal, do you, Kana?"

"Not unless they outlawed books over the weekend." Indeed, Kana had several books she'd borrowed from friends: *Living Like Zhuge Liang!*; *Warning of the Dolphins—So Long, and Thanks for All the Fish*; and *Marvels of Archeology: Did Moai Write the Dead Sea Scrolls?*

"As long as you're not smuggling a bomb or guns," quipped Kyouko.

"Give me some credit. What kind of idiot brings weapons to school?"

There was a great commotion from the front of the line, where the teacher, Miss Eri Kagurazaka, grilled one of the students.

"Do you really think you can get away with something like this on your first day here?"

"No, ma'am. I don't mean to cause trouble."

"Until you show me the contents of your bag, you may not enter the building."

"But . . ."

Although the boy seemed unnaturally calm, he also emitted an air of immense confusion and a desire not to be the center of attention.

"Who's that? I've never seen him around before."

Although he had the same stand-up collar as everyone else, he maintained a real sense of mystery about him.

It was safe to call the boy handsome, but his tight-lipped mouth and alert eyes indicated an extreme sternness slightly undermined by his messy black hair. Although he was thin, he looked pretty athletic, as if he participated in an active sport, like judo.

"Just open the bag, bub!"

Fed up, Ms. Kagurazaka slapped the bag out of his hands.

"Wait . . ."

"What do you have in here, anyway? I'll bet there's cigarettes!" She thrust open the bag, pushing aside notebooks, textbooks, and a smattering of writing utensils—and uncovering an Austrian-made automatic handgun with three ammo magazines. There also was a tube of explosives, several detonators, some stun grenades, a tiny camera, and a length of piano wire.

"Young man!"

"Yes ma'am."

"I don't know what school you came from; but around here, we confiscate toys like these."

"Excuse me?"

"Please wait in the staff room. It's almost time for class!"

All the onlookers laughed and moved on their way.

"Gross—he's a military nut," opined Kaname. "That gives me geek chills."

"He looks like he might be interesting," declared Kyouko smartly.

Poor Sousuke Sagara. Though he was at home on any battlefield and had been raised in international conflict zones, on a high school campus, he was a clueless moron.

Perhaps the security is tighter here than I had guessed, thought Sousuke as he and Miss Kagurazaka walked through an empty corridor.

At first, when she asked to search his bag, Sousuke thought he might have failed the mission already. After his weapons were confiscated, he resigned himself to following the teacher to the basement, where he assumed they would interrogate and beat him.

But then, as all the students submitted to the search, he realized that it was routine.

Wait a minute. Does that mean that a lot of students bring small arms and explosives to class?

Sousuke quickly looked around, but he didn't see anything to support or negate the idea.

If all the students were armed, it would make the bodyguard mission a bit more complicated. That meant it was conceivable that anyone, even the volleyball team walking down the hall, could be carrying submachine guns.

Sousuke was not overly concerned, however, because Kurz Weber was in an M9 Gernsback, camouflaged in a grove of trees behind the school. If Sousuke called him on his miniature wristwatch radio, the M9 could be there in about ten seconds.

"Urzu Six, what's your status?" whispered Sousuke into his watch.

"Tired and hungry," Kurz replied into Sousuke's hidden earpiece. "Need beer."

Miss Kagurazaka continued to lead Sousuke briskly down the hallway. She was a proper-looking woman in her mid-twenties. She wore a short bob haircut and a tight-skirted gray suit.

"Ma'am," began Sousuke, "about that gun . . ."

"It will be returned to you at the end of the school term," she interrupted.

"That's not the issue. The problem is that there's already a round in the chamber. It's extremely dangerous, so please don't touch the trigger under any circumstances."

"Huh? Oh, okay."

"It's loaded with splat rounds that have an extremely high kill rate. So, even an accidental firing will cause fatalities. Handle it with caution, please."

"I understand. Don't worry."

She clearly did not understand. Against her instructions, Sousuke worried.

From their desks in the clamorous classroom, Kaname and Kyouko watched Miss Kagurazaka lead Sousuke Sagara into the room.

Kaname and Kyouko conducted a brief, wordless conversation through facial expressions and gestures.

Look, there he is!

The gun nut!

"Quiet down, everyone!" shouted the teacher, rapping the attendance book against the blackboard. "Take your seats and pipe down. It's time to meet your new classmate."

Obediently, the majority of the students quieted.

"Okay. Mister Sagara, please introduce yourself."

"Yes, ma'am." Sousuke took a step forward. "My name is Sergeant Sousuke Sagara," he boomed.

Almost immediately, he paled at his own idiocy.

"Surgeon So Gay Soggy Log?" called one of the jokers from the back of the room.

"Sir John Soaks a Saw Gulag?"

"Sergeant? Like an army sergeant?"

"Quiet everyone! Give the new student a chance to speak," the teacher ordered sternly, again tapping against the blackboard with her book to quiet the class down. "As for you, Mister Sagara, this is no time for jokes."

"I apologize."

Previously, Sousuke never had felt so nervous on a mission. The pressure was intense. Letting that one word slip could cause the failure of the entire mission.

Sweating profusely, he snapped to attention and started over. "I am Sousuke Sagara. Ignore the 'sergeant.' That is all."

"That's it?"

"Yes, ma'am. That is all."

Miss Kagurazaka turned to the class. "Any questions?"

"Where are you from, Sagara?"

"I have lived many places—Afghanistan, Lebanon, Cambodia, Iraq—but I haven't stayed in any one place for very long."

The class fell silent.

"Wow. Sounds like Mister Sagara moved around quite a bit," concluded Miss Kagurazaka. "If I'm not mistaken, you transferred here from America, right?"

"That's correct," said Sousuke, acknowledging his fake transfer papers, which showed a previous address in Fayetteville, North Carolina. Although Sousuke never actually had been there, he knew some people who had.

One of the students raised his hand, but he didn't wait for the teacher to call on him. "Got any hobbies?"

"Model guns!" offered someone from the back of the room, and the class erupted in laughter.

"I enjoy fishing and reading," Sousuke said truthfully.

Whenever Sousuke had time to spare at Mithril's West Pacific base, he dropped a line in the water and picked up a good weapons manual. Even when it rained, he sat out there under an umbrella, immersed in his own little world.

"What do you read?" inquired one of the students.

Sousuke's eyes lit up. "Primarily technical writings and specialized magazines, such as *Jane's Fighting Ships*, *Soldier of Fortune*, and *Arm Slave Monthly*. I also have read the Japanese *AS Fan*, which contains surprisingly high-level information. Lately, I've been completely captivated by a series from the Naval Institute Press . . ."

Sousuke realized he had lost a hundred percent of his audience already. He hung his head. "Never mind. Please, forget that."

No need to ask: No one remembered, because no one was listening. One of the girls near the front raised her hand.

"Um, who are your favorite musicians?"

This could be difficult—Sousuke rarely listened to music. He grunted as he recalled the CDs Master Sergeant Mao had given him before he left on his mission.

"Oh, yes—Hiroshi Itsuki and SMAP."

April 20, 15:08 (Japan Standard Time)
Jindai High School, Tokyo, Japan
Athletic Club Wing, 2nd Floor

"What a weirdo," exclaimed Kaname as she undid the ribbon on the chest of her uniform. "I mean, nothing he says makes any sense at all. I don't think he's trying to be funny, either—I think he's legitimately messed up in the head, a psycho."

As Kaname removed her blouse and put it on a hanger, she knocked over the baseball bat that had been leaning against her locker.

"Darn it! I mean, did you see him during class? He just kept looking around. And in between classes, he paced around in the hallway. So weird."

"Really?" asked Kyouko, who was in the process of removing her skirt. "I didn't notice."

"So weird. Seriously, it annoys me just to look at him."

"Then don't look at him."

"I-I wasn't," protested Kaname as she readjusted her bra. "Why would I look at a maniac like that? But this is the worst—the worst! A couple of times, I caught him looking at me. He played it like it was an accident and just looked away, but it was creepy. Creepy!"

"A lot of guys look at you, Kana. You're really pretty, you know," commented Kyouko with a tinge of envy. She pulled up her socks and reached for her orange softball pants.

"Thanks, but it's not like that. It's like he's up to something."

"You know, Kana, you've been ragging on Sagara nonstop."

"I have?"

With long strides, Sousuke crossed the school grounds, stopping in front of the athletic club wing. Surveying the building, he saw there were six windows in a row on the second floor. He located the stairs.

He went up.

"Yes, you have!" said Kyouko.

Kyouko knew Kaname very well—including that Kana was quite popular despite having a dangerous mouth and a very candid demeanor. She was generally very good-natured, so much so that she practically had been forced into the position of student council vice president.

For Kaname to criticize someone she didn't really even know—and to do it behind his back—well, that was a very rare thing, indeed.

"For someone you're not interested in, you sure seem to talk about Sagara an awful lot."

"Don't be ridiculous! It's not like that. Ha ha. Ha ha ha!"

As a longtime friend, Kyouko also understood that Kaname's laugh roughly translated to: "I don't know, but I don't want to talk about it."

"Come on. Let's go."

Having finished changing into their uniforms, Kaname and Kyouko started to leave the changing room, where there were still many girls in various stages of undress.

But just as they were about to reach the door, it crashed open violently.

Eighteen changing girls looked into the eyes of the student in the doorway: Sousuke.

There were eighteen simultaneous gasps.

"Eeeeeeeeeee!" Shrieks rattled the windows.

Sousuke stood there dumbly, wearing a look of profound surprise.

Completely wasting a golden opportunity, he barely glanced at all the girls in their underwear. (Scantily clad women were only a distraction from the mission at hand, he knew.)

Springing forward, he grabbed Kaname and threw her to the ground. Somehow, by the time they hit the floor, he had drawn a pistol out of an ankle holster.

"Everybody, get down. Get down!" he yelled as he made a lightning-quick turn toward the open door.

He waited, gun trained on the doorway.

Nothing happened, of course.

Keeping Kaname pinned to the ground, he kept the gun pointed at the door. He surveyed the room and did not see anyone who appeared threatening.

Actually, upon second assessment, there were eighteen girls crowding around him with murder in their eyes.

Ten minutes later, the mayhem was over.

"I never suspected you to have something like *this*," said Miss Kagurazaka, inspecting the .38 caliber revolver.

"I apologize for the trouble, ma'am," Sousuke said meekly. He looked worn out; his uniform was torn, his face was scratched, his wrists were chained behind his back to a chair (with his own handcuffs, which the girls had found clipped to his belt).

He never liked interrogations.

"I'm confiscating this."

"Please—"

"Sorry, no exceptions!"

"Please unload it. Those are hollow point rounds—very dangerous."

"Oh, for the love of . . ." Miss Kagurazaka trailed off. Then, she stood up. "Miss Chidori, I'm leaving him in your custody."

"What?"

"I have a staff meeting. We're planning the class trip, you know. He definitely is to blame for all this chaos, so talk it over with the other girls and decide how to deal with him, okay?"

It was unclear whether the teacher trusted Kaname or simply was irresponsible. Either way, she was gone already. Sousuke, who regarded Miss Eri Kagurazaka the same way Cambodians viewed U.N. peacekeepers, was extremely disheartened to see her go.

Under the intense glowering of so many pissed-off young women, Sousuke had a good idea what was in store for him.

"The Geneva Accords state—"

"The what?"

"Never mind."

Kaname had no reason to know anything about those; she probably thought Geneva was the capital of Brazil.

"So, Sagara, what's the big idea? I mean, being a perv is one thing. But you'd have to be retarded to jump in here like a freaking commando! Are you mental or what?"

"'Mental'? You mean, 'smart'?" *How can I be retarded and mental at the same time? What is the meaning of this contradiction?*

Sousuke realized it didn't matter. Each second felt like eternity.

"You psycho! Look at this!" Kaname rolled up her sleeve. "See that? My elbow's all skinned up because of you. What are you gonna do about it?"

Sousuke assessed the damage. The skin was not broken, but it was a little bit red. The injuries Sousuke had sustained during the fray were far worse, but no one seemed to care about that.

Finally, he spoke. "It should heal very quickly."

"That's mean!"

"You creep!"

"A girl's injuries last a lifetime!"

"So, what do you have to say for yourself?"

"Apologize to Kana."

Sousuke felt like a tank caught in crossfire. As far as he could tell, it appeared they did not appreciate his actions.

"I'm sorry for violently handling you," said Sousuke. "But please let the record show that it was not my intention to cause you or your friends any harm."

"Then, what *were* you doing?"

"I'm afraid that information is classified."

"What do you mean, 'classified'? Tell me!"

"No, I'm sorry . . ."

Pushing her bangs off her forehead, Kaname said: "Tell us why you came here in the first place."

Thinking quickly, Sousuke answered, "I want to join the club."

None of the girls knew how to respond to that.

"I was a member of a similar club at my last school. I'm very proud of my participation, and that's why I was hoping to join. I'm confident in my physical strength and think you will only benefit from including me. So, what do you think?"

Internally, Sousuke commended himself for the bold delivery of his impassioned plea.

"Look, Sagara," began a flustered Kaname, "this is, well, it's the *girls'* softball club."

Sousuke processed this information. "So . . . boys can't join?"

"Of course not!"

"I think the circumstances warrant an exception, don't you?"

Fed up, the girls picked up Sousuke, chair and all, and kicked him down the stairs.

April 20, 18:45 (Japan Standard Time)
Chofu, Tokyo, Japan
Tigers Apartments #505

On a display screen, a black-haired girl opened the door to her apartment and went inside. After she swung the door shut, there was the gratifying sound of a lock clicking into place.

"Eighteen-hundred forty-five hours. Angel is safe at home. No shadows," reported Melissa Mao into a walkie-talkie-like device.

She toggled the display to see what Kurz was up to with the AS. She couldn't see Kurz, of course, because of the ECS, but she knew that he would be running along the road and probably would be back in a couple of minutes.

Mithril's intelligence bureau prepared a base for their mission—a safe house of sorts. Just across the district line, they had a good view of Miss Chidori's apartment.

Their room didn't have any real furniture—just a cheap table and some folding chairs. Still, the apartment was pretty full, loaded up with small weapons and surveillance equipment.

"I can't get over how expensive everything is here in Tokyo," grumbled Mao to no one in particular. She polished off a hamburger; then, she pulled out her menthol cigarettes, firing one up.

Shortly after that, Sousuke entered.

Mao laughed out loud when she saw him. His hands were chained to a strange-looking chair, which he had been dragging behind him the whole way.

"Oh, Sousuke, you made a friend!"

"It's a chair."

"I can see that. Why are you dragging that old thing around?"

"Because I can't get the handcuffs off. They're a hinge model, and the keyhole's pointed toward my elbow."

"Give me a break," Mao chuckled as she pulled out her own master key and undid the cuffs.

"Thanks," said Sousuke. Then, he related the details of the day.

" . . . and that's what happened. Buying a subway ticket at Sengawa Station was the most difficult part. What's the matter, Mao?"

Pinching the top of her nose between two fingers, she said, "It's nothing, just a little headache."

"Oh. Perhaps you should rest a little."

Interrupting that thought, a small electronic sound signaled a transmission from Kurz. "This is Urzu Six, done for the day. Does one of you want to switch with me?" he pleaded.

The M9 was safely inside a makeshift hangar, an oversized-trailer in a nearby parking lot.

"Are you sure no one saw you, Kurz?"

"I almost kicked an old man. Every dog in a two-mile radius barked its head off. I nearly smashed up a pachinko parlor. I stopped to rest against an elementary school and cracked the windows. You should've seen the little dudes freak out."

At any rate, no one *saw* the M9. With a less-skilled pilot, the near misses might have ended in disaster.

"Maybe this isn't the best way to go about this, after all," suggested Mao.

"If we stick to the plan around the clock . . . then, yes, it may be impossible," agreed Sousuke. "I think it would be best to have the AS on standby here, starting tomorrow."

"It seems like such a waste of its firepower and sensors, though," reasoned Mao.

Because the M9 was the absolute latest in AS technology, it was fully equipped with electronics that cost tens of millions of dollars. Its audio-detection system operated a "smart filter" that alerted the pilot to potentially dangerous phrases, such as "take captives" or "weapon discharge permitted." On top of that, the M9 had two machine guns that easily could take out twenty to thirty unarmored vehicles.

In hindsight, the M9 might have been a little bit too extravagant for the mission at hand. But Mao came from the most extravagant military in the world—the U.S. armed forces.

"I want the M9 as close to Kaname as possible. As long as we avoid rush hour and move along the river, I think we'll be okay."

"I trust your judgment," declared Sousuke.

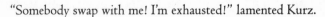

"Somebody swap with me! I'm exhausted!" lamented Kurz.

"Wait a minute. Miss Chidori's getting a phone call." Mao twiddled some knobs on her equipment and offered Sousuke a spare headset. "Want to listen?"

"I suppose."

The caller was Kaname's little sister, who lived on the east coast in America. They had a friendly chat, touching on many subjects, including the "crazy new transfer student," who she described as "pretty entertaining, at least." When it came time for her to hang up, Kaname seemed a little bit reluctant to end the call.

"Poor girl, living all alone," said Mao, sympathetically. "I guess she gets only one dose of family a day, through a long-distance call."

"I'm not sure I understand completely," said Sousuke, "but a scheduled communication is a good idea." He thought about this for a minute. "It's strange, though. In my dealings with Miss Chidori, she was a lot sharper, more aggressive."

"Of course, she was different—she was talking to her little sister."

"Is that typical?"

"Yes."

"Noted. I'm also surprised to learn that she doesn't totally despise me."

"You sound pretty excited about that, Sousuke."

"Do I?"

Sousuke turned to the window and studied his reflection for any traces of elation.

April 20, 11:30 (Greenwich Mean Time)
Pacific Ocean, Depth: 165 Feet
Amphibious Assault Submarine Tuatha de Danaan

"Sergeant Sagara sure seems to be having a tough time with this mission," said the girl in the captain's chair, who, according to appearances, was only in her mid-teens.

The young woman had large gray eyes and braided ash blonde hair that hung down over her left shoulder. She wore informal clothes—a stylish brown suit that was two or three sizes too large.

Regardless, a captain's rank insignia sparkled on her collar. And although the awards and decorations common to most captains were nowhere to be found on her chest, the girl, Teletha Testarossa (a.k.a. Tessa) was captain of the Tuatha de Danaan.

Captain.

Only a small group of people knew the reason why.

One of them, Lieutenant Commander Kalinin, stood beside her in the submersible's command center, which was about the size of a small theater. It was the Tuatha de Danaan's brain, unifying the ship and its combat teams.

"It could be a valuable learning experience for him," opined Kalinin.

The young captain continued to scan the most recent report from Melissa Mao, which detailed Sousuke's adventures in a business-like fashion.

"Firearms confiscated. Assaulted by a gang of civilians, including the guarded target. Returned to safe house in exceedingly disabled state, tied to a chair."

"Nothing he can't handle, Captain."

"True, Mister Sagara is a top-notch sergeant. Even so, I'm glad he has Miss Mao and Mister Weber with him."

Tessa paused to look at the clocks—one for GMT and one for JST—on her display screen.

"Lieutenant Commander? How long do you think those three will have to be in Tokyo?"

"It could be several weeks until we locate and suppress the source of the threat, Captain." In spite of his physical seniority, Kalinin responded with immense respect.

"So, it all depends on the progress of our mission," concluded Tessa as she studied a marine chart on the display screen. "If everything goes according to plan, we will eliminate the need to guard Kaname Chidori."

"As well as the rest of the Whispered candidates."

"For the time being, at least."

"Yes, unfortunately."

Kalinin excused himself; then, he saluted and left.

Meanwhile
Soviet Union
Outskirts of Khabarovsk

Two cars sat parked atop a lonely bridge that straddled a frozen river. Apparently, all noise in the outlying area also had frozen solid, as it was dead quiet.

Three men stood in the center of the bridge: one Asian man in a fancy Italian coat and two Russians, both clad in KGB uniforms.

"Too quiet," grumbled the Asian man, adjusting his slicked hair. There was a large scar on his forehead—a remarkably straight line that resembled a knife's slash or a bullet's kiss. It looked almost like a third eye.

"Quit whining; you're the one who designated this meeting place," said the more corpulent of the two KGB men, a colonel according to the decorations on his shoulder.

"I was referring to the activity between your ears. I can hear the moths' wings flapping!"

The colossal captain next to the colonel lunged forward. "What'd you just say?" The colonel restrained him.

The Asian man laughed. "At least the colonel has decent people skills."

"It is not our error," protested the irritated colonel. "The Whispered test subject was stolen, and there's a good chance they got their hands on the candidate list, too. Without a test subject, we can't conduct the research; it's as simple as that."

The colonel sounded irritated—and with good reason. The research he spoke of was being conducted without permission from the party's central committee. If they detected his unauthorized activities were a failure, he most certainly would be sent to a labor camp.

"So Gauron, are you through investigating the enemy's objective?"

"More or less. Take a look," said the scarred man, handing the colonel a photograph. "I ran an image enhancer on this photo you gave me."

In the photo, there was the vague outline of an AS.

"It's using ECS—that's why the outlines are blurred as if they're melting into the surroundings. It appears to be carrying a backpack, maybe transporting VIPs up that mountain slope."

The AS looked slick, remarkably similar to a human. Impressed, the colonel raised an eyebrow. "What is this? I'm not familiar with this type."

"It's a Mithril AS," Gauron cheerfully responded, "much too advanced for you to worry about it."

"Mithril?"

"It's a secret organization of mercenaries. Their equipment is a good ten years ahead of the rest of the world: top guns, elite soldiers. You haven't heard of them?"

Mithril was an enigmatic force, perpetually present in the shadows of international conflicts. They attacked armed guerilla bases and destroyed drug-manufacturing plants. They allegedly annihilated terrorist camps and prevented nuclear-weapon smuggling.

Mithril's mission was to extinguish the flames of regional conflicts. Consequently, they weren't on any particular side.

"Why would they interfere with my project?" asked the colonel.

"Probably because it's dangerous. If you were to succeed, it would upset the world's balance of power."

"So, they're going to make it hard for us to capture a new Whispered candidate, I suspect."

Having one of the Whispered girls in their custody was absolutely essential to their project's success. Now that theirs was lost, they simply would have to find another.

"I can abduct one, but it'll take some time—it's more trouble than killing one," said Gauron.

"Does that mean an increase in your fee?" growled the colonel.

Smiling, Gauron said, "I'm a businessman, not a communist."

"Very funny, you yellow monkey!" shouted the captain. "You're completely replaceable! How about you show some thanks to the colonel who keeps hiring you, anyway?"

"I am thankful for your patronage," responded Gauron.

"You Chinamen are all empty promises!" roared the captain.

"What an insightful comment. I'm not Chinese, though," corrected Gauron.

"Either way, you're all the same! Wait until I send you to the Ural mountain coal mines and turn your grinning yellow face black! You puny pig!"

"You, sir, are very annoying."

With the skill and speed of a card shark, Gauron pulled a pistol from under his coat. It was such a smooth and simple action, it looked as if he were pulling out a cell phone.

The red point of a laser sight dotted the captain's forehead.

A gunshot shattered the nighttime quiet.

Blood, skull fragments, and pieces of brain littered the snow. The captain's body, with the surviving half of his head, clattered to the ground with a thud.

"Now, where were we? Oh, yes! Discussing the terms of the kidnapping," Gauron nonchalantly put away his pistol. He looked at the case file the colonel had given him earlier.

"Ah, here. This is it," said Gauron. "Is there a problem, Colonel?"

"That's one of my men . . ."

"But really, you just brought him here to intimidate me, *da?*" said Gauron, cruelly. "At least you don't have to babysit him anymore. Now, let's get down to business."

Speechless, the colonel let the madman take the wheel of the conversation.

Rifling through the documents, Gauron counted roughly fifteen separate files with the personal information of fifteen Whispered candidates. Judging by the photos alone, the boys and girls were different nationalities and races but all roughly the same age—mid- to late teens.

"Now, which one do you want me to get? I know, I know—it's already decided. You want," Gauron shuffled through the papers, "this one! Hey, she's pretty cute."

To the colonel, Gauron presented a photograph of Kaname Chidori.

Chomping on fries from the burger joint beneath the department store, Kaname and her friends gabbed merrily.

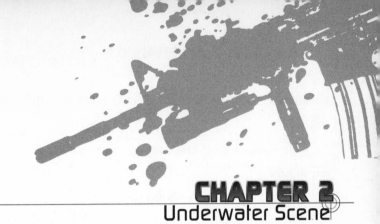

CHAPTER 2
Underwater Scene

April 23, 17:32 (Japan Standard Time)
Chofu, a suburb of Tokyo, Japan
Keio Line, Chofu Station, South Entrance

Of course, Sousuke tailed her, keeping an eye on the situation from the opposite corner of the shop. Sousuke looked around nervously while pretending to read a three-day-old copy of *Tokyo Sports.*

Sousuke didn't like the look of the man sitting at the counter behind Kaname—mid-twenties, medium build, eyes hidden beneath a plain gray beret. The man had a black attaché case at his feet, and he incessantly checked his wristwatch.

What's in the case? wondered Sousuke.

It reminded him of one he had seen in a catalog of anti-terrorist equipment. If his memory was correct, that particular model had a built-in submachine gun, which could be fired at the flip of a switch.

After polishing off his hamburger, the man stood up with his tray in hand.

Here we go . . . Sousuke readied himself for action.

But the man simply deposited his hamburger wrapper in the trash, placed his tray on top of the garbage can, and left.

So I was wrong. Unless . . .

Sousuke looked and saw the man's case sitting on the ground, where he'd left it. *What if . . . Dammit!*

It was not unheard of for terrorists to blow up a whole crowd of people to get at a particular target. But wasn't Kaname supposed to be a *kidnapping* target? Maybe the situation changed. At any rate, Sousuke didn't have time to think about it.

He dashed through the cramped eatery, upsetting tables and shoving diners. He grabbed the briefcase, which was certainly heavy enough to be a bomb.

However, this action didn't go unnoticed. "Sagara?" said Kaname in disbelief.

"Get down!" shoving away more customers, he charged out of the hamburger joint with the mysterious case.

Now, where can I get rid of this thing?

Sousuke surveyed the surrounding area—during the evening, the shopping district was positively crammed with people. He spotted a parking lot across the street—perhaps there would be fewer people there.

"Move!" yelled Sousuke as he bolted out into the street, angering drivers literally left and right.

Honk! Honk!

Sousuke turned just in time to see a truck squealing to a halt. It couldn't stop in time, and it sent Sousuke flying. He crashed into a bicycle stand on the side of the road.

Failure . . . not an option . . .

Standing up as quickly as his woozy head would permit, Sousuke was in the process of trying to relearn how to walk when the suspicious man from the burger place approached him.

"Hey man, are you okay?" inquired the man, relieving Sousuke of the attaché case. He popped it open. "Oh, thanks. I don't know what I would have done if I had lost my manuscript."

The man slapped Sousuke on the back and left.

A small group of people, including the truck driver, Kaname, her friends, and some other passersby, stood staring at Sousuke. Some were worried, some confused, some amazed, but all seemed to be expecting some kind of explanation.

"What on Earth are you doing, Sagara?" wondered Kyouko.

"I thought it was a bomb," Sousuke said meekly before collapsing on the pavement.

April 23, 19:20 (Japan Standard Time)
Chofu, Tokyo, Japan
Tigers Apartments, #505

"At this rate, you'll be dead by the end of the week!" Kurz laughed as he wrapped a bandage around Sousuke's head. "You're probably more dangerous than any terrorists! Try to relax a little."

"I'm trying," said Sousuke.

That evening's hamburger-hut fiasco was just the icing on the cake of four days' worth of misguided efforts with catastrophic (and injurious) results.

No matter how hard he tried, Sousuke could not stop himself from overreacting—acting violently, crashing around, destroying public property, disturbing class—and Eri Kagurazaka and Kaname never let him forget it.

He never ran out of energy or fresh bruises.

Even in the harshest combat conditions, Sousuke hadn't ever taken so much abuse in such a short period of time. He fell down stairs, crashed through windows, crumpled beneath a falling pile of books in the library, and chafed his chest while tackling a plaster art model, among other things.

My rhythm is totally off, he realized, unsure how to correct the problem. How ironic that he was able to survive so many years of intense combat only to be undone by high school!

"You can't keep up this pace," decided Kurz. "Tomorrow, we'll switch. Mao and I will keep watch outside the school."

"What if the enemy comes inside the school?"

"I doubt that will happen. I wonder whether Kaname's really a target even."

"Wishful thinking is dangerous." Sousuke couldn't help but frown at Kurz's easygoing attitude. "You always must take every possibility into account—"

"If you want to get hit by a truck," interrupted Kurz. "Have you ever heard the expression 'tilting at windmills'?"

The look on Sousuke's face indicated that he had not.

"Hm. It's like a sumo fighting against his own loincloth."

"Loincloth?"

"You don't know that one? Are you even Japanese?" Kurz finished wrapping the bandage and returned to the window. "There's one thing I don't understand."

"About loincloths?"

Kurz rolled his eyes.

"About Kaname. She seems so . . . normal. I mean, she's pretty but not, like, jaw-dropping hot. And her personal history is very commonplace—compared to ours, at least."

"You might be right."

If Sousuke learned nothing else from this mission, he'd at least discovered the startling difference between others his age and him.

"So, why is she a KGB target? It's just like that girl we picked up last week. She was just a normal high school student before they snagged her, too. What the hell could they possibly stand to gain by taking and drugging these girls?"

"All I have is the same information you do," said Sousuke.

"Yeah, there must be something more to this than the lieutenant commander's telling us."

April 23, 21:21 (Western Pacific Standard Time)
Khabarovsk, Soviet Union
KGB Building

"When are you going to get moving?" demanded the KGB colonel. Three days had passed already since his meeting with Gauron.

"Soon, very soon," answered Gauron through the other end of the phone.

The colonel could hear bustling in the background. Gauron—a terrorist of unknown origins—was calling from the Soviet embassy in Tokyo. According to official embassy reports, Gauron barely left the building and rarely spoke to anyone.

"I'm making the arrangements now. We have to make sure everything's in place before we move in on the target."

"Arrangements? What kind of arrangements do you need to make?"

"Don't be so impatient."

"What?"

"There's no way Mithril's just going to let us waltz right in and grab her."

"You mean they're protecting Kanumu?" The colonel still struggled to pronounce her name.

Chuckling, Gauron said, "It seems so. If I'm not careful, I'll be noticed."

"I don't care!" spouted the colonel. "Kill anyone who gets in your way if you have to!"

"I'm afraid that's impossible."

"Why?'

"They have an AS in ECS invisible mode that's keeping tabs on her."

"And no one has noticed? That's impossible. That kind of equipment—"

"I told you," Gauron interrupted antagonistically, "their equipment is ten years ahead of the rest of the world's. They probably have some of their best personnel on this mission, too. If we run in there like a bunch of amateurs, they'll embarrass us all."

The colonel stuttered.

"Don't worry, I've got a plan," Gauron stated and hung up. "You just worry about keeping yourself out of the labor camps."

April 24, 14:38 (Japan Standard Time)
Jindai High School, Tokyo, Japan
Year 2, Class 4 Classroom

"And there you have it!" Kaname finished scrawling a list of jobs on the blackboard.

She turned around to face a room full of disinterested students, who were sleeping, shooting craps, and reading manga novels.

"Hey! Listen up, guys!"

"We're listening," they all said automatically.

"We have only five days before the class trip. And we need to decide what job each person will do if we want the trip to go smoothly."

"Okay, fine. Let's decide and go home, already."

Kaname sighed. "Remind me why I agreed to be class rep," she moaned. "Well, I figured it would be like this, so I already assigned all the jobs. All you guys have to do is say whether it's okay."

A cheer erupted from the students. "Way to go, Chidori!"

"No problem," she said, flashing a quick peace sign. "Okay, Onda and Sanematsu—you're in charge of food. Aryiama and Omura—luggage. Onodera and Suzuki—event planning."

She scribbled names next to the jobs that already were written on the board. Suddenly, a slightly malicious grin crossed her lips. "And garbage duty . . . that's a job for Sagara."

At the mention of his name, Sousuke snapped out of his preoccupation and grunted.

"Is something wrong, Sagara?"

"I don't recall signing up for that."

"Sorry, it's a school rule—the transfer student always has to be in charge of garbage. Rules are rules."

Everyone laughed, but Sousuke didn't get the joke.

"I wasn't aware of that. Very well, I accept."

"Excellent. I'll fill you in on the details later. Okay everyone, all in favor?"

And just like that, Mithril's finest mercenary got elected to pick up trash through a unanimous vote.

April 24, 11:13 (Greenwich Mean Time)
Sea of Japan, Depth: 165 Feet
Tuatha de Danaan Command Center

"A class trip?" asked Captain Testarossa.

"Yes," said Kalinin, handing her a few documents and a pen. "The trip starts next week. I propose we open a new confidential circuit for communications during the trip. Also, please sign this permission slip."

She nodded and signed the document. "What a strange school, taking a trip at this time of year. Where are they going, anyway?"

"Okinawa."

"Oh." Tessa quickly turned away, staring at a map on her forward display screen. "Did you know that I used to live there?"

"No, ma'am."

"My father wanted me to go to a Japanese elementary school," she said wistfully, "but I never made any friends, and then I transferred to a school on the base."

Commander Mardukas, the ship's executive officer, cleared his throat, snapping Tessa back to earth.

"I guess this isn't the right time and place for memories," apologized the captain.

"Probably not, ma'am," said Mardukas before returning to his personal duties.

Kalinin kept reading his report as though nothing had happened. "We have new information."

"About the Whispered?"

"Yes, ma'am. Apparently, the Khabarovsk facility still is conducting research. Take a look at this."

Kalinin thrust the bundle of documents at Tessa. It appeared to be an endless list of chemical substances, marked sporadically with red circles.

"The circled substances rarely are found in the USSR," explained Kalinin. "According to our intelligence—"

"Is Khabarovsk the only research facility?" asked Tessa, interrupting Kalinin.

"It's the only one our intelligence division reports."

"That's questionable. Please request a continuation of the investigation."

"Yes, ma'am," Kalinin asserted as if he himself hadn't already ordered the investigation.

"Is there any way for us to disable the Khabarovsk facility remotely—maybe with computers?" proposed Tessa.

It was a good thought; the de Danaan's computer system was head and shoulders above a regular warship control system. Its processor was almost as powerful as that of a large mammal. This system ran circles around the American military's communications system. Cracking Soviet computers would be no problem with this beast of a machine.

"Unfortunately, the research facility computers are cut off from outside circuits," said Kalinin, effectively bursting the bubble. "We'll have to physically disable the laboratory."

"I see. Cruise missile?"

"Yes, ma'am," assented Kalinin. "A G-Type Tomahawk will suffice. It should be a straightforward strike from a fuel-air-explosive warhead."

Captain Testarossa considered this for a moment; then, she looked at her map. The scientists lived less than one mile from the lab. "Okay. But let's minimize the casualties—do it at night, the next time they take off a day. For now, gather the latest photos from Sting and get as many details as possible. Who, what, where, when."

"Understood. Now, regarding the Arbalest . . ." Kalinin let another handful of papers finish the sentence for him.

As he handed them to Tessa, she dropped the huge stack of papers she already was cradling.

"How clumsy. I'm so sorry," she squeaked as Kalinin and Mardukas helped her corral the loose sheets.

"Thank you, Mister Mardukas," said Kalinin.

"No problem," said Mardukas, implying moderate annoyance. "Seriously, though, Lieutenant Commander, you should use electronic documents like everyone else."

"I'll figure it out, eventually," said a visibly flustered Kalinin as he handed the captain the document.

"The Seven Oaths of Garbage Duty?" read Tessa.

Embarrassed, the lieutenant commander quickly took back Sousuke's report and handed her the correct documents.

April 25, 16:35 (Japan Standard Time)
Suburbs of Tokyo, Japan
Keio Line, Hasimoto-Bound Train

"This is the last straw!" announced Kaname, disgruntled.

After carefully placing a bookmark into her worn paperback, the young woman stood and moved briskly toward the other end of the train car, where Sousuke sat, pretending to read a sports newspaper.

"Hey," demanded Kaname, "you got a problem?"

"Oh, Chidori. What a coincidence."

"Yeah right," she said before snatching the newspaper from his hands and taking a quick look at the headlines. "What is this, anyway? You're reading old news!"

"That's my prerogative."

"Why are you following me around?"

"I don't know what you're talking about. You must be overly self-conscious," Sousuke stated matter-of-factly.

"I'm not self-conscious. You're harassing me—all day, every day! If you want to say something, just say it and quit being creepy!"

"As I said, it's purely a coincidence."

Kaname took a moment to process this assertion. The train conductor made an announcement over the loudspeaker, doing his best impression of a boxing announcer.

"Ladies and gentlemen! The next stop is Kokuryou Staaaaaation!"

Kaname tossed Sousuke's newspaper to the floor, startling an old lady nearby. The train lurched to a stop and the doors whooshed open, signaling the arrival at Kokuryou Station.

"So, it's all just coincidence?" checked Chidori.

"Yes."

"If you say so."

Right as the door started to close, Kaname dashed through it onto the station platform.

She thumbed her nose at Sousuke, who began to panic. "See you later, weirdo!"

The train began to move forward.

As Kaname walked toward one of the benches, Sousuke suddenly crashed through one of the train's windows, landing back first on the platform. He bounced a couple of times, and then he rolled before finally smashing into the iron fence at the edge of the platform.

"Are you kidding me?"

Sousuke lay there like a slug, unmoving. Kaname rushed to him, kneeled, and gently shook him by the shoulder.

"Hey, are you okay?" she wondered.

After a moment, Sousuke jumped up as though nothing had happened. "No problem. Just a little dirty."

He wiped the dust off his pants.

"Are you crazy? What were you thinking?"

95

"I just remembered that I . . . I wanted to get off at this station. It had nothing to do with you."

"After that display of insanity, you still want to insist—"

"Just a coincidence."

Sighing, Kaname drooped onto a nearby bench. Sousuke took a seat next to her and pulled out his sports newspaper, which he had retrieved somehow before leaping from the moving train.

"And it's just a coincidence that you're going to read that paper right here?"

"Correct."

"Unbelievable." Kaname rested her elbow on her knee and her head on her hand, staring at Sousuke all the while.

Oddly enough, his behavior didn't strike her as particularly creepy. True, since he'd transferred in, he had stared at her, walked into her locker room, and followed her pretty much everywhere she went every single day. Even so, she didn't really suspect him of being a stalker.

Something was different about him.

Sousuke didn't seem to harbor any indecent feelings or have a discernibly impure motive for following her around. He looked too dignified to be a deviant.

Like an athlete before a match, he radiated determination and purpose. He looked calm but remarkably focused and deep in concentration.

So, why the hell was he following her?

"Hey, Sagara."

"Yes?"

"If I promise I won't get mad, will you at least tell me what's going on?"

"There is nothing going on, aside from a string of coincidences," he answered in his typical, business-like manner.

"Right, right," she conceded. "Well, seeing as you're here by coincidence, may I ask you something?"

"Sure."

"You lived overseas for a long time, right? Were you always this weird at all your other schools?"

For a moment, Sousuke considered the question. "Yes, I suppose. Those were peaceful and uneventful days."

"Were you sad to leave your friends behind?"

"No. I still keep in touch with them via telephone and written correspondence. So, it would be inaccurate to say I've left them behind."

Kaname rolled her eyes.

"It isn't difficult."

"Is there a girl?"

"I know many girls," Sousuke did not understand where this was going at all.

"No, a *girlfriend*," pressed Kaname. "You know, a sweetheart."

"I have no friend like that. One of my colleagues—my 'friend,' if you will— always says, 'There isn't a yak in Tibet that would be your girlfriend.'"

Kaname laughed. "Your friend is funny."

"I don't even know what that means."

"He's just saying you're really weird, Sagara."

"Weird?"

"Extremely," snickered Kaname. "But that's not necessarily bad. You just need to find a nice person who finds it endearing."

"I'll keep that in mind. You know, you seem like a nice person," he remarked.

"Stop it. Don't take it so seriously. I'm not talking about me," she protested.

"Okay. Never mind, then."

"You really are weird," joked Kaname.

For a moment during their conversation, she had felt a faint warmth, similar to how she might have felt if she'd found a stray dog whose only desire was to follow her everywhere she went. Temporarily, her loneliness was buried beneath the pleasantness.

I guess this is nice, for now . . . she thought.

A train rolled into the station and interrupted Kaname's thought process.

April 25, 19:05 (Greenwich Mean Time)
Sea of Japan, Periscope Depth
Tuatha de Danaan

Just enough moonlight pierced the water's surface to keep the submarine cloaked in shadow.

From an outside perspective, the Tuatha de Danaan looked kind of like a shark, except it was several hundred times as large. In fact, the assault submarine was as big as a skyscraper turned on its side.

The giant submarine moved through the water quietly—very quietly.

Near the rear of the sub, one of the missile tubes opened and a missile emerged.

Kicking up a healthy, foamy spray, the Tomahawk missile erupted into the air and spread its cruising wings. Shortly thereafter, it reached a steady altitude and rocketed on toward the northern horizon.

"Launch sequence complete. Closing MVLS hatch," announced the officer in charge of the Missile Vertical Launching System.

"Excellent," declared Tessa, glancing at her command screen's safety indicators. "Now, let's dive to three-hundred thirty feet and change course to the south."

"No problem, Captain," responded Commander Mardukas, a tall, thin man, whose black-rimmed glasses and pallid, bony features made him look more like a scientist than a soldier.

"Let's go, then," urged Tessa. "Flood the main ballast tank and set the submersion angle to ten degrees. Increase speed to ten knots."

Tessa, a submariner with more than ten years of experience, gave the orders without timidity, even though she was still relatively new to the Tuatha de Danaan, inarguably the most high-tech submarine in the world.

Tessa knew that launching a cruise missile potentially could attract a lot of attention, so it would be best to vacate the area as soon as possible. They could use Mithril's spy satellite Sting to see whether they hit the target.

"Aye aye, ma'am," said the navigation officer. He echoed her orders as he performed the tasks.

"Will it really take three hours to know the outcome?"

"Yes, ma'am. Perhaps you should rest," recommended Mardukas.

Tessa shrugged. "That would be nice, but I'd probably have nightmares, anyway."

At any rate, the missile was on its way. If the attack succeeded, it probably would take the enemy five years to recoup. Arduous recon from the intelligence division indicated that Khabarovsk had the only Whispered research facility in the country.

"Lieutenant Commander, if we can destroy the laboratory, will we recall our guards?" asked Tessa, sinking into her chair.

"Yes, ma'am. However . . ."

"Yes? What is it?"

"Nothing. I'm probably just being paranoid," said Kalinin, looking somewhat troubled.

April 26, 10:38 (Western Pacific Standard Time)
Khabarovsk, Soviet Union
KGB Building

"The whole laboratory is in a state of ruin!" shouted the colonel into the phone. "A missile attack, of all things! All our data is gone. We've lost every single piece of information on the Whispered."

Gauron's unsympathetic voice leaked through the phone. "I'm sorry to hear that."

"Resuming our research is impossible, so we no longer will need the girl."

"I see. That's a pity."

"Yes, you must cancel the abduction; there's no way we could pay you." The image of Gauron killing a man in cold blood flashed through the colonel's mind.

"I understand," Gauron said calmly—a little too calmly.

"Do you really?" probed the colonel.

"Of course."

"You seem awfully calm, considering your source of income is gone."

"I have many jobs," stated Gauron. "I'll go back to another employer, maybe even bring him a souvenir."

"Souvenir?"

Something clacked against the receiver.

"Do you know what that was, colonel? That was a DVD I found. Sounds like a good one, huh? It has all kinds of fascinating figures on it."

"The research data? How did you—"

"Trade secret, comrade. Be sure to write me a letter from whatever labor camp the KGB dumps you in. Goodbye, Colonel."

Click. Knock! Knock! Knock!

The colonel looked to the door. Before he could say anything, three armed soldiers burst through.

"Colonel Smirnoff?" asked a young lieutenant. "Your side job intrigued the party headquarters. You are accused of dispersing national assets to your personal accounts, resulting in a substantial loss for the nation."

"Wait, that's not—"

"Save your explanation for Lubyanka. This way, please."

Lubyanka. Russians knew the true meaning of this word and feared it immensely. Lubyanka meant intense interrogation and life in a labor camp. Just like that, Colonel Smirnoff's fate was sealed: a world of nothing but agony awaited him.

The colonel hung his head as the soldiers led him away.

April 26, 20:01 (Japan Standard Time)
Chofu, Tokyo, Japan
Tigers Apartments, #505

Deservedly, Sousuke took a day off, spending all day resting in the apartment.

That Sunday, when Kaname left her home at noon, Kurz tailed her, Mao piloted the AS, and Sousuke monitored Kaname's apartment.

Throughout the entire day, not a single suspicious person appeared. At one point, a middle-aged woman with a child rang the buzzer to Kaname's apartment, but she proved harmless.

Shortly after eight p.m., Kaname returned home safely.

"Twenty-hundred hours, six minutes. Angel is home. Nothing unusual," said Sousuke into his microphone.

Right about then, Kurz burst through the door of the apartment, glowing with good cheer.

"Heeeeeeeere's Kurzie! Ha ha. What's the deal, Sergeant Moody?"

When Kurz spoke, Sousuke could smell the beer on his breath. Sousuke kept his eyes glued to the surveillance monitor.

"Honestly, Kurz. Drinking during a mission?"

Kurz laughed meekly. "What can you do? I was going to have just one, but Kyouko kept insisting."

"Kaname's friend Kyouko?"

"Yeah. When I saw Kaname, Kyouko, Yuka, and Shiori, I told them I was lost. 'Thank you so much! You saved me! Japanese girls are so nice!' Cute too. Ha ha!"

What Kurz lacked in stealth, he more than made up for with confidence.

"For God's sake, smack some sense into that idiot," crackled Mao's voice through the wireless receiver. She was back in the trailer with the AS.

"It isn't my fault they're so cute!" protested Kurz. "Besides, it was nice to see some girls other than a certain bitchy someone who will remain nameless."

"Kurz, this is classified guard duty. You don't want to become too attached," reminded Sousuke.

"Are you mental, bro? Getting up close and personal makes it that much easier to keep tabs on them. Obviously."

"If you become attached, it can cloud your judgment. In order to maintain a rational power of observation—"

"Yeah, in theory!" interrupted Kurz. "In times of great danger, you have to use your head, feel it out a little bit."

"But . . ."

"Am I wrong?"

Sousuke stared dumbly at Kurz, unable to say 'yes' or 'no.' He wasn't even sure what point he was trying to refute anymore.

"Man, those girls talked my ears off," began Kurz. "'There's a really weird transfer student in our class, right Kana? Isn't he weird, Kana? Tell him about the new kid, Kana.' I can't believe they didn't want to talk about important things . . . like *me*."

Suddenly, Sousuke perked up. "What did they say about me?"

"I see. So, you want to know, do you?" Kurz gloated.

"Not really, no. But it's part of the mission, so I should hear it."

"Not buying it. First, say, 'Please, sir, tell me some more.'"

Sousuke was not amused.

"Okay, fine. You don't have to be such a baby about—" spotting something suspicious, Kurz suddenly became very sober.

He moved closer to the surveillance screen.

"Twenty-one hundred twenty-one: suspicious individual on the balcony side. Commencing investigation," reported Sousuke.

The monitor showed Kaname's apartment's balcony, courtesy of a hidden camera on the roof of an adjacent building. On the left side of the image, a man clad in black and a knitted mask scaled the building's drainpipe.

"Is he stupid enough to go alone?" remarked Sousuke while screwing a silencer onto a nine-millimeter handgun.

"Dunno. There still could be others nearby. I'll check cars in the area," said Kurz, grabbing a nearby sniper rifle with a night vision scope.

"This is Urzu Two," said Mao, through the wireless. "Let's subdue the perp. Urzu Six, take that rifle to the roof where the camera is."

"Urzu Six, roger."

"Urzu Seven, subdue him directly. I'll be in the parking lot, keeping watch."

"Got it. Give me two minutes."

Slinging rappelling gear over his shoulder, Sousuke rushed out the door.

One-hundred twenty seconds later, he was on the roof of Kaname Chidori's apartment building. He clipped the rope to the railing and nimbly wound it around his waist. Kurz's voice came through his earpiece.

"This is Urzu Six. I'm in position by the camera. There's no sign of accomplices. He actually might be flying solo."

"Don't let down your guard, especially at your six."

"Who do you think you're talking to, bonehead?"

Mao interrupted their banter. "Perfect timing, Urzu Seven: Kaname's in the shower. Let's try to take care of this before she comes out."

"Urzu Seven, roger."

"Don't kill him."

"I know."

And just like that, Sousuke threw himself off the roof. Aside from the slight whisper of the rope sliding through his hands, he was silent. After bounding down the wall a couple of times, he was directly over the prowler's head.

The intruder was so focused on climbing over the railing onto the balcony that he didn't even notice Sousuke.

Taking one last leap off the wall, Sousuke skillfully twisted in midair and crashed down on the back of the man on the balcony.

"Don't move." Sousuke pressed his silenced gun against the back of the intruder's head. "You lose. Don't make a sound."

Shaking violently, the man nodded.

"Good, you value your life."

Keeping the man pinned to the ground, Sousuke conducted a brief body search. The pat down turned up no weapons, only a wallet. Sousuke took a look at it.

Inside, there was a student ID.

Jindai High School, Year 2, Class 4, #10. Shinji Kazama.

This boy was in Sousuke's class.

"Urzu Six to Urzu Seven."

"What?"

"Sousuke, look at what he's holding."

Sousuke saw what appeared to be several small pieces of cloth.

"Panties," smirked Kurz. "White as fallen snow. End transmission."

Sousuke looked over to see Kurz laughing and packing up his gear.

"For crying out loud," grumbled Mao as she retreated in the camouflaged M9.

"What are you doing, anyway?" demanded a confused Sousuke. He pulled off the prowler's mask.

The boy underneath—thin, childlike, and pale—trembled with fear.

"I'm sorry, I'm so sorry, I'll never do it again!"

"Shh!" hissed Sousuke, pressing the gun tighter against the boy.

Much quieter, the boy said, "Sorry. Please don't arrest me."

"I'm not the police," clarified Sousuke. "I just want you to explain yourself."

"You won't arrest me?"

"Relax." Sousuke pulled the boy to his feet.

"Thanks. Hey, you're from my class. Sagara, right?"

"You must be mistaken."

"No way! You're—"

Sousuke cocked his gun. "I said, 'you must be mistaken.'"

Nodding feverishly, the boy apologized.

"Now, Kazama, right? What are you doing here?"

Holding out the underwear, Shinji Kazama said, "As you can see, I'm on a panty raid—looks like we had the same idea."

"No, I was just in the neighborhood," fibbed Sousuke.

"Oh. Right." Though confused, Shinji didn't try to argue.

"Why on Earth are you trying to steal Miss Chidori's undergarments?"

"They're not for me," whispered Shinji. "Murano and the others—"

"Murano?" inquired Sousuke.

Shinji Kazama revealed the situation.

Every school has its share of delinquents, and Murano was Jindai High School's chief hooligan. He and his goons knew that Shinji was in the photography club, and they pushed him around and stole some of his negatives. They would give them back only in exchange for Kaname's underpants.

"So, you're being blackmailed?" iterated Sousuke.

"More or less." Kazama sighed. "But those guys really aren't *that* bad. They just wanted me to prove that I had enough guts to steal underwear from the most popular girl at school."

The convoluted plots of deviants never failed to strike Sousuke as immensely ridiculous. "I see. Did you ever think that Miss Chidori might be rather upset?"

"Well, yeah," admitted Kazama guiltily, "but I really want those negatives back."

"What's on them?"

"Arm Slaves. All different kinds, but U.S., Japanese, and self-defense models mostly."

"Oh yeah?" Suddenly, Sousuke was quite interested.

"Yeah, I went around to bases all over Japan to take those pictures. It was a ton of work, too. Isn't AS technology one of your hobbies, Sagara?"

"I wouldn't exactly call it a hobby . . ."

"I've even got a picture of a Marine M6 in Okinawa."

The M6 first saw combat in the early '90s, most prominently in the Gulf War. Once people saw it on the news, it became an extremely popular piece of equipment.

"Was it the A2 model?"

"Yeah. It had a shield with reactive armor and everything."

"Really? How were its actual movements?"

"The operators at the base said the balance wasn't great," Shinji reported. "That makes sense, because its control system is the Rockwell-built MSO-II, right? The feedback architecture has a lot of flab, so when the bilateral angle exceeds three point five, it's even susceptible to handheld firearms."

Sousuke nodded, acknowledging all the jargon.

"Basically, its best use still would be a well-plotted ambush or a suicide charge. I read somewhere that the newest model M9s are still a long way off from widespread use . . ."

As Shinji rambled on about technical mumbo-jumbo, the two young men sat cross-legged on the balcony. Their military geek discourse soon buried all memories of the foiled underwear theft.

"Your knowledge is impressive. You don't sound like a civilian at all," praised Sousuke.

"There's still so much to learn," said Shinji modestly. "You sure know a lot, too, Sagara."

"Thanks, but—"

Clattering, the balcony curtain opened, interrupting Sousuke's attempts to be demure.

Sousuke and Shinji's eyes grew to the size of dinner plates.

Kaname stood in front of them, frozen with fright, rage, or some combination of the two. Her bath towel barely concealed her shapely chest, and it covered even less of her legs.

Tightly clutching her towel, Kaname demanded to know what was going on.

As Sousuke and Shinji struggled to explain themselves, Sousuke realized he harmlessly had been playing with a pair of underwear.

His eyes traveled from the damning cotton evidence to Kaname and back.

"Chidori!" he chirped. "What a coincidence."

Quietly, Kaname disappeared into her apartment.

Shinji and Sousuke shared a sigh of relief.

And then, she reappeared—with a metal softball bat in hand.

"That's one hell of a bruise, buddy!"

Kurz wrapped a sack of ice around Sousuke's arm.

"I believe she intended to kill us. Kazama got lucky—I distracted her just long enough for him to leap into the shrubs below."

"From the fourth floor?"

"Yes. He plunged into the cherry tree and to the ground from there."

"Were you trying to kill him?"

"I was lucky to get away. Imagine the lieutenant commander's disappointment if the girl we're supposed to protect had ended up killing me."

Kurz laughed. "Actually, I can totally picture his expression."

Knowing the lieutenant commander's stoic disposition, he probably would sigh once, fill out some forms regarding the distribution of the deceased's possessions, and then move right on to the next job. Lieutenant Commander Andrei Kalinin never seemed particularly surprised by any person's death.

"She'll probably *really* hate me from now on," complained Sousuke.

"I don't blame her, you perv," joked Kurz.

A moment later, Mao contacted them from the M9. "Guys, I was just on the horn with the de Danaan."

"New orders?"

"Yes. The mission's over: The enemy no longer has any reason to kidnap Kaname."

"What do you mean?"

"We blew the crap out of the base where she was wanted. We annihilated everything, including all their research data. That means we can relax for a while."

"Huh. So, do we go back to the ship now or what?" asked Kurz.

"That's the best part. We get to take a week off!"

"No way! Yes!" whooped Kurz, raising his hand for a high five.

Sousuke just sat there, looking disgruntled. "I was supposed to go on a class trip the day after tomorrow—five days and four nights."

"He said you should," Mao cleared her throat to do her best impression of Kalinin, "'Go and have a good time.'"

"The lieutenant commander said that?"

"Yeah. We already paid for the trip. We're to stick to the budget. Looks like it's an order."

"But—"

"Just go, Sousuke," said Kurz, who abandoned all hopes of a high five. "Relax. Kaname's safe, so just take a load off and try to act like a normal kid for a change."

After thinking it over for a moment, Sousuke said: "Okay, I'll go. It will be a valuable learning experience."

April 28, 09:15 (Japan Standard Time)
Haneda Airport, Tokyo, Japan
Passenger Lobby

Although he was under direct orders to "have a good time," Sousuke was not in the best of spirits. Free of his mission's obligations, he was more than a little bit uncertain what to do with himself.

On top of that, Kaname really seemed to hate him this time. When their eyes had met by chance, Kaname simply had turned around and walked off in the other direction with Kyouko and the other girls.

"Well, you really can't blame her," lamented Shinji Kazama from his perch on the airport bench. "I mean, she did find you out on her balcony, having a chat with her panties in your hands."

Ever since the incident, Shinji and Sousuke were associates in shame, complicit in embarrassment.

"Hey, cheer up, Sagara."

"Right." Sagara looked forward to returning to the Tuatha de Danaan and receiving another assignment.

Why did he agree to go on the school trip, anyway?

"Okay, Class Four!" announced Miss Kagurazaka. "Have your tickets out and your IDs ready!"

Sulking, Sousuke and Shinji moved through the line and onto the plane.

Having seated a whole plane full of rowdy students, the stewardess breathed a sigh of relief. Actually, there were about eighty or so passengers that weren't part of the school trip. And as those passengers began boarding the plane, they already were rolling their eyes in anticipation of the students' youthful energy.

Visions of future headaches flashed through the stewardess' head. She grimaced.

"Hello?" called a passenger as he stepped through the door. "Can you tell me where my seat is?"

He waved his ticket in front of her.

"Yes, please follow me," she said, forcing a smile.

"I can't say I envy you, having to babysit all these students."

"It really isn't that bad," she said.

"I would snap for sure, probably toss them all out the window at twenty-five hundred feet."

Somewhat confused, she grunted.

"If we killed them all, we'd have a quiet flight, don't you think?"

"Sir, it isn't—"

"I'm only kidding," he explained, quite seriously. "Ah, there it is."

The man smiled as he slid into his seat, but it was not at all a pleasant smile.

119

April 28, 09:58 (Japan Standard Time)
Air Over Tokyo, Japan
JAL Flight 903

The jumbo jet reached its cruising altitude.

Having never been on a plane before, Kyouko gripped the side of the window and pressed her face against the glass. It was a bright and clear day, and she could see all of Tokyo.

"Wow, look! Hey, there's the Rainbow Bridge. Awesome!"

"There it is," Kaname said halfheartedly.

"Are you even listening, Kana?"

"Of course."

"Look, the Statue of Liberty!"

"Yep."

"The Eiffel Tower!"

"Neato," monotoned Kaname.

Kyouko nudged her. "What's the matter? You've been acting really weird all day. What happened?"

"Nothing, really." Kaname didn't feel like explaining that she was mad at herself. She thought she might learn a little bit about this Sagara character when he jumped out of the train window to follow her, but all she found out was that he was a geeky, moody, perverted stalker!

It was stupid of me to trust him, she thought glumly.

"Is it about Sagara?" guessed Kyouko.

"What? Of course not. No way. Ha ha. Ha ha ha!"

Despite Kaname's obvious use of her nervous "let's talk about something else" laugh, Kyouko had no intention of dropping the subject.

"Did he do something to you?"

"No, not really."

"I knew it. I mean, it was just Sunday that you said he actually might be a nice guy; but the very next day, you totally ignored him. What did he do?"

"Nothing, really."

"Come on, Kana. Even if you're scared to tell anyone else, you can tell me." Kyouko took Kaname by the hand. "You'll need to go to the hospital, too. I'll go with you."

"Hold on—"

"Don't worry—we'll make Sagara pay for this! I know this lawyer who deals with this kind of thing a lot. She's good, too."

"What are you blabbering about?"

Before Kyouko could answer, the plane pitched left and right, rocking back and forth. Kyouko let out a small yelp.

"It's okay, nothing to worry about," stated Kaname coolly, although the plane's swaying hadn't totally stopped. "It's weird, though, I've never been in turbulence when the weather's this nice."

Students, natural gossipers and conspiracy theorists, were buzzing about the bumpiness. Kaname tapped the student in the seat in front of her.

"Hey, what's going on?"

"I don't know. But I swear I heard some kind of popping sound just before the jolt."

"Popping?"

Ding!

"Attention, passengers. Don't be alarmed. We've encountered a low-pressure system. We've adjusted our course. We still may encounter future turbulence, but I assure you that there is nothing to worry about."

Ding!

"That's strange," Kaname decided.

Confused, Kyouko asked why.

"I mean, they don't usually say 'don't be alarmed.' Usually, they say 'please fasten your seat belts,' or something like that."

And neither one of them knew just how right she was.

CHAPTER 3
Bad Trip

"Good. We don't want the passengers to panic."

Setting down the little microphone, the pilot stole a look at the smug bastard with the laser-sighted pistol standing behind him. The man's black hair fell over his forehead, nearly covering his large scar.

"I can't believe you used an explosive on the plane! Are you nuts?"

"It was just a small one—barely big enough to get into the cockpit."

"You're lucky you didn't blow us all to smithereens!"

"Probably true," responded Gauron in a very chilling voice. "Hey, stick to the course!"

White with fear, the pilot ran his eyes over the gauges. "The electrical system took a hit in that explosion. We're in danger if we don't make an emergency landing."

"Is it broken?" The terrorist inquired, attempting to decode the complex instruments.

"It is. We'll negotiate for your demands, but if we don't return to Haneda Airport, we'll probably crash."

"I think I see what's broken," said Gauron. "It's this, right here."

And he pointed the gun's laser sight at the pilot's head and pulled the trigger. The firing of the bullet made less noise than the sound of flesh and bone ripping apart. The pilot died instantly.

"I see. It's beyond repair!" chuckled Gauron.

"What've you done?" moaned the copilot, who now was wearing a considerable portion of the pilot's cerebral cortex. The little red laser dot flickered across the copilot's face.

"You're not broken, too, are you?"

"Don't shoot! No one else can fly the plane!"

"I must admit, I've always wanted to get behind the wheel of one of these things," laughed Gauron, invading the copilot's personal space. "Tell me, is it as fun as it looks?"

"Please, don't kill me."

"I just asked if it was fun, stupid."

Painfully slowly, Gauron's finger tightened around the trigger. Just as he was about to squeeze it, another large man entered the cockpit.

"Gauron!" barked the man, who was nearly six and a half feet tall. He wore a suit and glasses but didn't really resemble a businessman.

"Hello, Koh."

"Why did you kill the pilot?"

"He lied to me and tried to make me look foolish."

Very nimble for his size, Koh grabbed Gauron's gun. "Who's going to fly the plane?"

"I'll do it; I fly transport planes all the time."

"They're not the same thing. Regardless, I thought you were supposed to bring only a knife."

"A knife? How barbaric. *Please.*"

Koh grabbed the jeering man by the lapels. "Look, it's your business if you get off on murder. But don't forget, you're working for *me* and *my* country. If you jeopardize this . . ."

"Don't worry. I'm a perfect gentleman," protested Gauron, "as long as people listen to me. Right?"

He clapped the terrified copilot's shoulder. "What's your name?"

"M-Mouri."

"Mister Mouri, as you may have heard, I'm not supposed to kill you. But, if you don't do as I say, I have no problems killing other people until you learn to listen. Got it?"

"Please, don't kill anyone."

"That all depends on you."

Gravely, Mouri nodded, gulped, and focused on flying.

"I didn't tell your dead *amigo*, but I have people all over this plane. And they're all armed. Just keep that in mind."

"How did you ever get all those weapons on board?"

"I'm organized. I had a little help from one of the maintenance workers."

"You b-bribed them?"

"More or less." Gauron cracked an evil-looking smile.

In actuality, Gauron had kidnapped the man's family and coerced him into doing what he wanted. Then, for good measure, Gauron cleaned up the mess to prevent future trouble.

"Now then." Gauron abruptly pulled out a map. "Take her right along this route."

The copilot paled. "North from MIMOD? We're going to Sunan? Isn't that North Korea?"

"Very good, you get an A in geography."

"They'll shoot us down."

"I wouldn't worry about that. Just follow our directions to the letter, and they'll even escort us in. They're not as precise as we are," griped Gauron, "but go ahead and use the ILS system, anyway. Once we pass this point, broadcast your identification."

And Gauron continued to lay out the details of the plan.

It took a while for the authorities to realize the full gravity of the situation when the plane entered Naha FIR, changed course northward, and flew into South Korea's Daegu FIR.

A debate arose among the Ministry of Transport as to whether Flight 903 merely was experiencing mechanical problems or if it had been hijacked.

During the most heated part of the argument, the South Korean Air Force phoned in the settlement—they just received word that the plane was, in fact, hijacked.

However, the message had to pass through all kinds of different channels and translators, so it took the Ministry of Transport almost twenty minutes to get it.

Finally, the Security Council took over handling the situation.

Meanwhile, Flight 903 carried on right into North Korea. The South Koreans called off their aerial pursuit and were more than a little surprised to see that no North Korean planes arrived to intercept the jet.

The Metropolitan Police Department had an anti-terrorist force called SAT, but there wasn't much they could do now that the plane was all the way in North Korea.

Out on the campaign trail, the Prime Minister learned of the incident during a press conference when an NHK reporter asked him about it.

Shrugging, he commented that he didn't have any information and would talk about it as soon as he did. He then, perhaps foolishly, resumed talking about other topics, giving his critics much fuel.

The strangest aspect of this hijacking was that no one claimed responsibility for it.

The U.S. AWACS in South Korea issued an announcement that Flight 903 landed at Sunan's Air Base, about twelve miles north of Pyongyang.

And the whole time, the hostages were ignorant of their predicament.

April 28, 11:55 (Japan Standard Time)
Democratic People's Republic of Korea
Sunan Air Base

Something was amiss.

The passengers did not understand why they had been flying over mountain ranges for so long, nor why they weren't already to their island destination.

The stewardess was just as in the dark as everybody else.

"No need to worry," she assured them, smiling, "I'm sure we'll be landing soon—probably has to do with the weather."

Eventually, the plane did prepare to land. Passengers on the port side of the craft could see a town near the runway, but it looked quiet and rundown, lined by old-fashioned factories belching puffs of nasty black smoke. Looking out the window was like looking into a picture of Japan's past.

"I knew something was wrong," asserted Shinji Kazama. "This isn't Okinawa. It doesn't even look like Japan."

"It would seem that way," replied Sousuke.

During the flight, Sousuke and Shinji easily identified the South Korean Air Force F-16. They knew there was no way that plane would be flying over the Pacific Ocean en route to Okinawa.

Before long, the plane landed. Several hundred feet from the runway, there was a large hangar in which many outdated warplanes sat, waiting for action. The aircraft looked like carps with wings glued on.

"Sagara, those are MiG-21s. I mean, J7s."

From their vantage point in the plane, they also could see a pair of antediluvian tanks.

"Whoa! Look at those! T-34s!" Shinji nearly crapped his pants. "Those junk heaps are at least fifty years old!"

There were, in addition to the outdated technology, at least a few Arm Slaves. Sousuke and Shinji could make out three.

"Whoa! A new Rk-92! Did they skip everything in between?"

The Rk-92 was a long-armed, Soviet-made AS with khaki-colored armor and weapons, the most popular camouflage in the East. Most Western militaries referred to the Rk-92s as "Savages." Sousuke knew that AS well, for he had piloted one—even fought in it.

Based on the number and type of weapons, Sousuke knew it had to be, without a doubt, a North Korean base.

What is going on here, anyway?

According to Mao's latest report, Kaname was no longer in danger. However, the latest *hijacking* suggested otherwise.

This could not be a coincidence. Whoever was responsible chose the most reliable form of abduction—with several hundred hostages, not even Mithril would leap to the rescue carelessly.

To make matters worse, they were definitely in North Korea, a country whose relations with Japan were, to put it mildly, strained. A rescue operation in a semi-hostile area would be much more dangerous. It was a new twist to an old-school hijacking.

"Nicely done," assessed Sousuke.

"Huh?" grunted Shinji inquisitively.

"Nothing."

There was almost nothing Sousuke could do. In accordance with school policy and airline regulations, he didn't even have a gun with him. Even if he did, it wouldn't have done him much good.

Other, slightly denser passengers started to connect the dots and began to clamor.

Ding!

"Attention, passengers. Thank you for flying with us today," said a male voice. "As you might have guessed, this is not Naha airport. Due to unavoidable circumstances, we have been forced to land at the Sunan airport in the Democratic People's Republic of Korea."

"What? Are you kidding?" shouted Miss Kagurazaka, the rarely fazed homeroom teacher.

"Just listen, ma'am," instructed Shinji.

"Next week, the imperialist American military and their South Korean puppets are holding joint maneuvers to intimidate the heroic People's Army. My brethren in the People's Army must quash U.S. imperialism, even if that means taking all you nice people hostage. Please, take a look out the windows."

Several hundred people pressed their faces against the Plexiglas to see armored vehicles, Arm Slaves, and uniformed soldiers surrounding the plane.

"They are here to welcome you. But if you do not follow our directions, or if you foolishly try to escape, they will shoot you on sight."

Passengers gasped.

"Therefore, please remain where you are until the time of your release comes. The plane is equipped to accommodate you until your release. Thank you for your cooperation."

April 28, 04:05 (Greenwich Mean Time)
Korea Strait, Periscope Depth
Tuatha de Danaan Command Center

"We've been had," said Teletha Testarossa. "They've tricked our intelligence."

The command center's forward screen looked like a swirly finger-painting of information. Red, green, and yellow characters danced, complicated figures overlapped. Several different countries were mobilizing military units, and intercepted communications flew in from every angle.

"We're always a step behind," she lamented. "It's pathetic."

Reassuringly, Kalinin said, "Think of it as playing Whac-a-Mole. Sometimes, there's nothing you can do but wait until one shows its ugly head."

Tessa knew that Kalinin must have been at least a little suspicious, seeing as it was his idea for Sousuke to go on the trip. But even he seemed surprised by such a brazen and audacious move.

"Whoever is behind this, it sure doesn't seem like the KGB," determined Kalinin.

"Yes, and despite their location, I don't think North Korea's behind it, either," said Tessa.

"Right, ma'am. They're both just along for the ride with whoever masterminded this whole escapade."

Although they thought the research data was obliterated completely, someone must have salvaged it somehow. And whoever made off with the data had to have some kind of ties to North Korean military circles, as well as a research facility to exploit Kaname.

"Any guesses who Mister X and friends might be?"

"No idea at this stage."

"The North Korean government issued a statement that it is not responsible for this hijacking, as if it just fell into their laps. However, they seem pleased to have some leverage to stop the U.S.-South Korea joint maneuvers," reported Tessa as she finished reading the latest transmission from Sweden. She was quite adept at reading incredibly fast while talking about something entirely unrelated—a feat impossible for an average brain.

"So, Lieutenant Commander," she began, "what do you think are the chances the hostages will be released peacefully?"

"Excepting Chidori, you mean?"

Tessa nodded. "Right. If we don't make any bad moves, we might be able to negotiate the return of the other four hundred people on board."

"Yes. I suppose the North Korean government certainly doesn't want to add to the tension here. I mean, they had an abundant harvest last year, just started working on a palladium reactor, and have started to dig their economy out of the basement. They really don't have anything to gain by letting several hundred Japanese students die."

"Right. We should let their leaders deal with returning the hostages. Then, we can find and rescue Chidori."

Even if, for argument's sake, that plan would work, they knew exactly what kind of treatment Kaname would be subject to until that rescue.

Kalinin noticed the faint look of self-loathing that appeared on Tessa's face, but he pretended he hadn't.

"This makes sense, however—"

"We'll watch over things for now," interrupted Tessa.

"Very good. We still have some time. What should we do about combat standby?"

"Put transport planes on standby at the Merida Island base— three C-17s. And get a KC-10 in the air in two hours or less. We'll come up with the flight plans as necessary."

"Aye aye, ma'am," responded the communications officer before getting to work.

"Remember, Lieutenant Commander, we still have Mao and Weber," reminded Tessa. "Let's have six M9 Gernsbacks and three FAV-8 Super Harriers prepped and ready by oh-seven hundred. And—"

Tessa weighed the final decision in her mind before speaking. "Let's get the Arbalest into a usable state."

"Aye aye, ma'am."

"Let's not worry ourselves, now. We are prepared for situations like this."

Kalinin nodded and said, "Plus, the enemy's unaware of his deadly cargo."

Indeed, in a situation like this, Sousuke was undeniably dangerous.

"True. Let's wait for him to contact us," decided Tessa. "Keep the ship at periscope depth."

April 28, 17:18 (Japan/Korea Standard Time)
Sunan Air Base, Democratic People's Republic of Korea
JAL Flight 903

Despite the gravity of the situation, the students on the plane were abuzz with excitement.

The other passengers on the aircraft sat gravely awaiting new developments, but the Jindai High School students revolted against boredom with all kinds of raucous behavior.

Intense Hanafuda and mahjong card battles erupted. LIFE and Monopoly spread out across some of the seats.

Some of the students were yukking it up with handheld karaoke sets, some were getting a head start on the class-trip tradition of telling dirty stories, and some were racing remote-controlled cars up and down the aisles. The stewardess' head pounded so hard, she was nearly ready to make a break for it. The teachers tried to maintain some semblance of order; but the kids were so rambunctious, they had no choice but to give up.

"Hey, Kana, are you hungry?" asked Kyouko as they worked through a game of Old Maid.

Kaname watched Kyouko draw a particularly terrible card; then she said, "Yeah. I wonder when we'll be able to get some food."

"Maybe there's a convenience store around here," suggested Kyouko. "I'll just give you the money, and you can go out and get some food, okay?"

"Ha ha. Even if there was a shop around here, it wouldn't be Lawson, it'd be Il-Sung. Ew!"

"What's wrong with Il-Sung?"

"You don't know? What is wrong with young people these days?" joked Kaname. She turned around and looked at the seat behind her.

Sousuke Sagara sat nearby, quietly thinking.

That's how he reacts to an emergency like this? What the hell is the matter with him?

Absentmindedly, she pulled a card from Shouko's hand: a joker.

"Crap!"

"Oh, that's really a shame. Too bad," said Shouko.

Suddenly, silence rippled through the plane's cabin. Three men who had accessorized their suits with submachine guns entered the passenger compartment. A fourth man also entered; he was empty-handed and smirking. He fixed the collar of his expensive-looking suit and magnanimously spread out his hands.

"Carry on. Don't mind us!"

Only a handful of the most brazen students resumed their activities. The smirking man whispered something to the other three men, issuing instructions.

"What's this all about?" Kyouko asked uneasily.

"You, there," he called; it was the same voice they'd heard over the loudspeaker earlier.

Who was he talking to?

"Perhaps you didn't hear me. You, the pretty girl with the long hair."

Kaname sat blankly, unsure how to respond.

"Yes, you." He came closer and looked down at Kaname. He had a large, straight scar on his forehead, and his eyes had the same glassy lifelessness of a doll's.

"Can I help you?" Kaname asked.

"We're making a little video to send to the press, and we need someone to star in it."

"Oh, I see. I don't think I'm really cut out for it. I mean, I'm just an ordinary girl," protested Kaname.

"Nonsense. You're perfect for the role. Just come with me."

"But—"

The three goons with guns grabbed Kaname and brought her to her feet.

"Hey, let me go! Find someone else."

"Kana!" screamed Kyouko.

Heroically, or perhaps foolishly, Eri Kagurazaka laid into the man with school-teacher ferocity. "What do you think you're doing with my student?"

"We're just going to borrow her for a minute. We'll bring her right back."

"I won't allow it. If you have to take someone, take me," insisted Miss Kagurazaka.

"It wouldn't be as effective. We need—"

"Don't make excuses, you coward!"

The man's face coldly registered the verbal abuse.

"Who do you people think you are, anyway, hijacking a whole plane of people? Despicable! And now, you want to kidnap a *child?* Your morals are garbage! Whatever reasons you have for doing this, you can be sure—"

Smiling, Gauron pulled a pistol from under his suit. The little red laser rested on Miss Kagurazaka's forehead. "You talk too much."

"What? Please—"

Heedless, the terrorist slowly tightened his grip on the trigger.
BANG!

Everyone in the passenger cabin flinched as the sound resonated through the plane.

However, it wasn't a gunshot, just metal clanging. Everyone turned to look for the source of the sound.

A male student slowly picked up a tray and fork from the aisle.

"Excuse me," said Sagara, and he sat down as if nothing had happened.

Gauron stared at Sousuke, scrutinizing him. Sousuke kept his face down, silently staring at the cup in his hands.

Like prairie dogs, the students rose above their seats and looked back and forth from the man to Sousuke.

"Hmph," said Gauron, quickly losing interest. He put the pistol back under his coat. "Let's just go. We have what we need."

The terrorists headed for the exit, dragging Kaname past her gaping teacher.

Realizing how close she'd been to dying, Eri Kagurazaka fainted.

Students rushed to her aid, shouting for doctors. Calmly, Sousuke pushed his way through the plane until he reached the galley, where he placed his hands on the sink and finally breathed a huge sigh of relief.

Idiot.

It was far from sane to purposely attract the enemy's attention. But in the moment, he had known it was the only way to save Miss

Kagurazaka. His mind had fought its own battle. He knew it was not his duty to protect his teacher, but he also felt the very pressing desire to save her.

In the end, he did not understand why he chose to compromise himself to save the woman.

When the enemy had stared at him, it seemed to last an eternity. Masking his fury in a calm, albeit slightly ruffled exterior took every bit of Sousuke's willpower.

It's a miracle that he didn't recognize me.

Taking a moment to collect himself, Sousuke stretched his back. He would have to act quickly: Kaname Chidori was in the enemy's hands now.

I must respond to the situation.

There were no soldiers standing guard inside the plane—they mostly lurked around the outside of the plane, making sure no one exited. The plane was out of fuel, so there was no risk of it simply taking off. And there was no way of contacting the outside world, considering that Gauron had destroyed the plane's long-range communication equipment. Indeed, the jumbo jet made a great prison.

Sousuke needed to break out.

If he could just make it to his own luggage, he would be able to contact his allies and resume his search for Kaname.

Being careful to make sure no one was looking, Sousuke crawled into the galley elevator and lowered himself down a shaft into the cargo hold.

Cutting through the darkness with a penlight from his pocket, Sousuke searched through the large containers of luggage.

After looking through at least a dozen large containers full of bags, he found his own. He discarded the change of clothes and toiletry set; eventually, his hands found what he wanted—a high-powered satellite communication device with an attached codec.

Happily, Sousuke also retrieved a twenty-thousand volt stun gun from the bag. It was enough to incapacitate an average man with just one zap. He thrust a few survival items into his pockets and lamented failing to pack any guns or knives.

As Sousuke slung the gear over his shoulder and started to close the container, a shrill noise caught his attention.

Somebody was opening the luggage-loading door!

Quickly, Sousuke closed the lid to the container and hurried away, making a dive into the shadows of a large stack of bags as several men shuffled through the door.

Sousuke really wanted to look at the men, but he opted to remain safely hidden, instead. All he could do was bury himself farther into the pile of bags and try to breathe less conspicuously.

Of course, the men headed right toward him—purposefully, with guns clinking against metal belts. Sousuke counted: one, two, three men. He assumed they were trained for combat.

If they found him, he would have no choice but to fight, although he didn't like the odds of going at them barehanded.

And he didn't even want to *think* about how many men were waiting outside.

A Jeep carried Kaname to a remote corner of the base.

A truck and two large trailers sat atop what appeared to be an out-of-use apron. Loud, buzzing generators rested on top of the truck, enabling lamps to bathe the whole area in mercury-colored light. Several men with machine guns stood guard in front of the trailers, which resembled TV relay vehicles.

"Excuse me, what is this?"

Without answering, Gauron smiled and escorted Kaname from the Jeep into one of the trailers, which was chock-full of elaborate electronic and medical equipment: pods and wires, computers and doo-dads.

From a desk near one of the computers, a woman in a white lab coat watched Kaname enter. "Is that her?"

"Yes. Start the tests right away," said Gauron.

"Tests?" said Kaname. "What exactly—"

"Put this on," commanded the woman, handing Kaname a blue hospital gown.

"Why?"

"Your uniform has metal buttons on it," answered the scientist in perfect Japanese. "Also, if your bra has any hooks on it, you'll need to take that off, too."

What's going on here? Wondered Kaname. *And why do all the terrorists look Japanese?*

"Are you going to take an X-ray?"

"Something like that but much more advanced: PET, MRI, MEG from SQUID. We'll also need to take some NILS reaction measurements. At least, for now."

It was all Greek to Kaname. "I thought I was making a video."

"Hurry up and get changed," urged the woman.

"No. This is ludicrous! Why should I—"

Thwack!

A sharp pain ran through the nape of Kaname's neck, and she fell unconscious.

"That was taking forever," complained Gauron, holding the unconscious girl upright. "Now help me get her clothes off."

"Idiot! What if that affects the tests?"

"Don't worry about it. We just need to know whether she's the real thing."

The scientist mad-dogged Gauron. "You don't understand what the Whispered are or how important they are."

"I do so," insisted Gauron.

"Well, I suppose you may, considering you brought the highly classified Codarl with you."

"Even in its current unfinished state, I could take on a whole battalion with that thing. But it's just a precaution—in case our gracious hosts here change their minds."

"That's awfully cowardly of you. You must know your days are numbered."

Gauron let Kaname crash to the floor.

His right hand shot out and grabbed the woman's throat.

"Don't push your luck, sow," he said, brewing the perfect blend of coldness and joy. "Just be quiet and do the job you're paid to do. Do you like making me angry? Do you want me to hurt you? Huh?"

He tightened his grip on her throat until her eyes watered, and she choked out a wheezy, gasping cry of pain and ecstasy. Gauron clucked his tongue and deposited the woman onto her desk.

"When will we have results?" he asked the sputtering woman.

She hacked a few more times. "Tomorrow morning."

"Can you do anything to speed that up?"

"Even if we administer drugs, it'll be more than six hours before they take effect. Besides, there are preliminary procedures and examinations."

"Well, you'd better get to work, then," remarked Gauron, "or I'll have to kill you, too."

Luckily, the three men didn't notice Sousuke hiding, even though they passed close enough for him to reach out and touch them.

From his hiding place, Sousuke could see the back of their suits out of the corner of his eye. These were not soldiers from this base but terrorists from the plane ride.

"Where is it?" asked one of the men.

"It's around here—in the only yellow container. There it is!"

As they slid the yellow crate over, the ball bearings scattered on the floor, and a great rumbling noise filled the cargo hold.

"It won't just go off, right?" asked the most nervous-sounding terrorist.

"No. It's totally safe until the circuit's manually activated."

They pried the lid off the container, looked inside the box, and whistled.

"Wow! That's way bigger than I expected!"

"We didn't want to take any chances in case we had to use it on the ground. Okay, there should be a red cord near the back. Take the electric tape off the jack and insert it into the socket marked three."

"Right. Inserting."

"Hold on, I'm not ready yet. Okay, now: Stick it in there."

Click! Beep, boop, blip!

"Is that it?"

149

"Yeah, don't touch anything else. And don't use any hand radios in a one hundred foot radius."

The lid clapped shut, and Sousuke heard the men brushing off the cuffs of their suit jackets.

"Who all knows about this?"

"Just Sakamoto, the boss, and us. None of the locals know."

"Okay. It's really a waste—there are some really cute high school girls up there. It'd be nice to take a couple of souvenirs, you know. . . ."

"Don't be an idiot! The soldiers would notice and the boss would kill us all."

"The boss doesn't have to know!"

"I'll report you myself. I don't want the boss to kill *me*."

"Lighten up, I was just kidding," he said, and the three terrorists left the cargo hold.

Quickly freeing himself from the bags, Sousuke ran over to the yellow luggage container. After a slight pause, he opened the lid.

Shining his penlight on the contents, Sousuke confirmed his worst suspicions.

Those bastards.

It was a huge bomb.

To be more exact, the crate contained two tanks, approximately five feet tall, and most likely filled with binary liquid explosives—the same kind used in AS rifles. The side of the tank had a case with a small electronic circuit and a backup circuit. Sousuke interpreted its blinking red light to mean that it could be activated at any time.

If a bomb this large exploded, it would blow the entire plane to bits. With a flip of a switch, four hundred civilians would be toast.

Sousuke knew a lot more about bombs than a regular soldier, but he was no specialist. On top of that, he didn't have the proper tools for bomb disarmament. He knew that defusing this bomb was beyond his capabilities—in fact, he was far more likely to detonate it by accident.

Perhaps they want to slaughter the passengers to hide Chidori's abduction. It makes sense: If they return the other hostages but not Kaname, there would be questions.

I imagine they'll let the plane take off for Japan so they can blow it up somewhere over the ocean, where it'd be impossible to salvage any remains. No one would know that Kaname wasn't on board, and no one would ever suspect it was a kidnapping operation.

The plane crash would put the North Korean government in a tight spot—but not necessarily one that would develop into an armed conflict. The terrorists surely had taken all this into consideration when forming their plan.

But what reason could they possibly have to go to such great lengths to disguise their kidnapping of Kaname? Was she really harboring a secret worth the lives of several hundred civilians?

No, realized Sousuke. *That man enjoys pointless killing. That's why he'd think to do this.*

Closing the lid, Sousuke headed toward the nose of the airplane until he came to the little trap door that opened to let out the plane's landing gear. From there, he knew he should be able to exit the plane.

He had to find a way to contact the de Danaan.

The machine that held Kaname was creepy and coffinlike.

It was a cylindrical tube with acrylic walls. From time to time, the pedestal that held the machine would move, filling the tube with a thrumming noise.

A strap kept Kaname's head in place while special goggles spewed images of symbols and figures at her eyes.

Star. Circle. Square. Tree. Bottle. Rod.

Occasionally, an unpleasant image would pop into view.

Instinctually, Kaname yawned. It seemed like this had been going on for a long time, although it had been only about an hour.

"Don't fall asleep!" instructed the doctor.

"Right, right."

Kaname's thoughts returned to her situation. When she had regained consciousness, she already was strapped into the machine, wearing only the blue gown. Even her underwear was gone! The thought of that creepy, disgusting man seeing her naked made her want to kick and shout, but the female doctor had insisted that she was the only one present for Kaname's clothing change.

Reflecting on her current position, Kaname realized she probably should be more frightened. After all, she was alone in a time of crisis.

And that terrorist would have shot Miss Kagurazaka if that klutz Sousuke hadn't dropped his silverware right then.

It had been a long time since Kaname felt so near to impending death. The last time she had felt the sensation was while caring for her dying mother.

Acknowledging her own mortality, Kaname knew it easily could be her turn to go next.

I might not make it home. She reconciled herself with the thought.

In the corner of a storeroom that was at least a quarter of a mile from the jumbo jet, Sousuke eagerly extended his parabolic antenna. After checking the compass on his watch and mentally crunching some numbers, he adjusted the antenna and put on the headset.

Within five seconds, he was connected with Mithril's West Pacific base.

"Hello?" said a communications officer who was in charge of dispatching the calls.

Sousuke recognized her voice. "This is Urzu Seven of the de Danaan. Sergeant Sagara. B3128."

After a pause, the dispatcher confirmed his identity and asked if he was okay.

"Affirmative, Shinohara. Please connect me to the Tuatha de Danaan."

"One moment, please." And she reflected the satellite signal to reach the submarine.

"Mister Sagara! Are you okay?" asked the very familiar voice of Captain Testarossa.

"Yes, ma'am, Captain Testarossa," replied Sousuke, with much more formality than he would use to address any other girl his own age. He wasn't sure how Tessa had come to be Captain, but he understood the importance of her position and afforded her the utmost respect.

"Thank goodness! Hold on a moment, please. Lieutenant Commander!"

"Sergeant Sagara! This is Kalinin," he barked, as if Sousuke wouldn't have known. "What's going on there?"

"I'm at Sunan Air Base," reported Sousuke. "Although there are two separate opposition groups—the Japanese men who hijacked the plane and the local army—the security here is pretty low."

Sousuke then proceeded to describe in (perhaps excessive) detail the types and positions of the various weapons, the layout of the facility, and the whereabouts of the plane itself.

The officers were not surprised to hear that the terrorists took Kaname Chidori from the plane. Tessa did seem a little shocked, however, to hear about the bomb in the jet's baggage hold.

"Oh my God," she whispered.

"There's no way I can disarm it with the equipment at my disposal."

The Captain took a moment to process this. "Understood. We will consider countermeasures."

"Yes, ma'am."

"Sergeant, do you know where they're keeping Chidori?" asked Kalinin.

"Negative. I will search for her; but right now, I don't even know if she's still on the base somewhere."

"Well, keep out of harm's way. We'll need you to stay alive long enough to create a diversion."

Sousuke inferred that the de Danaan would launch a rescue operation and that his top priority was the plane passengers' safety.

"Roger."

"Thanks to you, we have a good idea of what we're up against. We'll need some time to mobilize, though. Can you contact us again—"

"At twenty-two hundred hours," suggested Tessa. "Local time."

"Roger," assented Sousuke. "One more thing, Lieutenant Commander, sir."

"Yes, what is it?"

"The leader of the hijackers—it's Gauron."

Sousuke could *hear* Kalinin's facial expression.

"He has changed somewhat since we fought him, but it was unmistakably him." Sousuke's use of the word 'we' predated his and Kalinin's time at Mithril.

"I thought he was dead."

"I did, too, but apparently he's not. There's a large scar on his forehead where I shot him before."

"Did he recognize you?"

"No, sir. Fortunately, my appearance has changed enough since then."

Sousuke remembered the days before his most-recent growth spurt, when his hair was long and wild, his skin dark from sun and grime.

"Okay, now the bomb makes more sense," decided Kalinin. "Don't let your guard down, Sagara."

"Roger. Urzu Seven out." Quickly dismantling his antenna, Sousuke rose to leave.

"Don't move," commanded a man with a slight accent, cocking his gun to emphasize the directive.

April 28, 20:32 (Japan/Korea Standard Time)
Yellow Sea, Periscope Depth
Tuatha de Danaan, Deck 3, Corridor B

"What was that about?" inquired Tessa as she walked with Kalinin toward the operations meeting room.

"You mean Gauron," he stated.

"Yes. Do you know him?" She stopped just in front of the door to the meeting room, waiting for Kalinin to answer.

After a moment, he spoke somberly. "'Gauron' means 'nine dragons' in Chinese. The dangerous terrorist we call Gauron is said to have nine nationalities. To date, he is responsible for at least thirty assassinations and two aircraft explosions, but he still is completely unknown to most Western anti-terrorist organizations."

At that point, Tessa recalled that Kalinin used to belong to a Soviet Special Forces group.

"Several years ago, Sergeant Sagara and I confronted Gauron. We were hiding from the KGB, allied with some Islamic Afghani guerillas."

It was not new information to Tessa that Andrei Kalinin got caught up in a huge KGB and Soviet military conspiracy—he still was considered a deserter.

"The KGB hired Gauron to find us. One day, while I was out, Gauron attacked the guerilla village with two Arm Slaves, nearly wiping it out."

Now, *this* was news to Tessa.

The AS was the mightiest present-day land-war weapon. Unlike tanks, they could go just about anywhere—jungles or mountaintops, it made no difference. In the face of this weapon, a human being was as powerless as an ant.

"Many died, including innocent women and children. If I had been there, though, it wouldn't have happened."

Understanding the heaviness of the situation, Tessa just nodded.

"And so I vowed retribution. Two weeks later, I got my chance. Gauron followed us to the mountains of Pakistan. We ambushed him, using me as bait and Sousuke as sniper. There were complications, but Sousuke brought him down,"

"Apparently only temporarily, though."

"So it seems."

Although she understood that Gauron was a brutal man, she still had a hard time swallowing the idea that anyone would kill several hundred people just to cover up a kidnapping. She certainly never would have thought of it if Sousuke hadn't warned them. She imagined Gauron sneering at everyone's optimistic hope that the hostages would return home safely.

"Well," Tessa surmised with an uncharacteristically cold smile, "I guess we'll have to make this Gauron character pay dearly for his actions, then."

"Yes, ma'am."

Although Tessa normally was a very gentle person, she ultimately lived in the same world as Kalinin and Sousuke—even the same world as Gauron.

She had to. After all, she controlled the Tuatha de Danaan, the most precise and powerful killing machine ever created by human hands. She had the power to kill millions of people if she ever had the need.

"We'll arrange the details later, Lieutenant Commander. First, let's commence with the operation meeting."

They opened the door and entered the dim room, where all six department heads already were waiting for them.

April 28, 20:33 (Japan/Korea Standard Time)
Democratic People's Republic of Korea
Sunan Air Base

"Turn around. Slowly."

Sousuke did as he was told, noting that the officer holding him at gunpoint was nearly six and a half feet tall, and he was quite burly on top of that.

"You're one of the high school students from the plane, right? I'm surprised you managed to get all the way over here without getting shot."

Keeping a safe distance, Sousuke relaxed a little. This officer was alone, and no one else was in sight.

"Who the hell were you talking to?" bellowed the ape.

"If you must know, I was in contact with—"

Sousuke interrupted himself, winging the transmitter at the man's face. It caught the man off guard; he barely managed to twist away, deflecting the transmitter at the last minute.

That split-second was all Sousuke needed to close the distance between them: He kicked the man's gun right out of his hand. It flew tantalizingly through the air before crashing to the ground.

"Wha—"

161

As if this were part of his daily routine, the huge ogre immediately heaved a wild punch at Sousuke's face. Although Sousuke blocked it, the punch had enough force to knock him backward.

As Sousuke took a single step backward, the man already had a roundhouse kick flying toward the sergeant's head.

Sousuke barely dodged the kick, but the giant's attacks just kept coming.

For his size, the man was ridiculously fast and skilled.

"Did you honestly think you could take me in hand-to-hand combat?"

As he fell back a few steps, Sousuke's rear foot found a concrete block. He leapt off the block, flinging a vicious jump kick toward the man's jaw.

With a grunt, the goliath toppled. His head smacked the asphalt, and his limbs splayed. Without delay, Sousuke pulled out his stun gun and zapped the man.

"B-b-bastard," sputtered the convulsing man.

This isn't working too well, worried Sousuke.

"Wh-wh-wh-who a-a-a-are y-y-y-you?"

"I'm the garbage man."

Finally, the man stopped struggling against the electric current.

Sousuke expertly bound and gagged him, using whatever materials he could scrounge from the storehouse; then, he examined his transmitter. It was cracked, and its circuitry guts spilled out. He flipped the switch a couple of times to no effect.

He would not be able to contact the de Danaan.

Uh-oh.

After collecting the unconscious man's pistol, Sousuke rifled through his first-aid supplies. The case contained sulfuric acid, aspirin, morphine, a syringe, some bandages, and a few other items.

Eventually, he found what he was looking for: a small bottle of alcohol.

According to Kaname's estimates, she had been in the cramped tube for several hours already.

It was so tight inside that experimental drum that Kaname couldn't move enough to alleviate the pain in her shoulders or back, and the frigid doctor ignored Kaname's requests for a break.

The whole time Kaname was in the chamber, images of unknown meaning flashed in front of her. Somehow, the doctor knew whenever the girl closed her eyes, as she immediately would yell at Kaname to keep looking ahead. The doctor had said that if Kaname focused, it wouldn't take as long.

Suddenly, the images ceased flowing, and Kaname was surrounded by blackness.

"Is it over?"

After a moment, a strange noise answered her question—a heavy, distant sound seemed to be coming from all sides at once. It made her nervous.

"What is this?"

Again, the doctor said nothing.

Images began to appear on the screen in front of her.

This time, they were words that changed every two seconds or so.

sea

campaniform sensillum

tree

intrinsic coercivity

decagonal phase

After a while, the pace picked up. Eventually, the nonsensical words came and went at a rate of ten per second. After that, the simple words like "tree" and "sea" stopped appearing, and there were only formulas and technical terms.

Kaname became aware that she was staring.

I recognize this. Where have I seen it before?

She wasn't familiar with the words, but somehow, Kaname comprehended their meaning. She understood the concepts better than the greatest scholars in the world.

Alloy of two-dimensional quasi-crystal structure, she thought, without knowing why.

> (Rugon and ninikke ∩ tachi Q tan. Type-I structural materials of ngoninna α frame. The 8 magnetocrystalline anisotropy which occurs in part bu stabilizer zirconia roriya 2 gu rare earth ion is non-linear ki a bure EK in Γ nona niki toshikuna. Praseodymium, terbium, dyspδrosium. No chi te Y poly Φ poly aru amide gel tomi ♪ bubbles, ju RG ze sechipu the C pliable na na naisharu muscles–)

Her thoughts knew no limits.

> (ΔD-T fu D fe GP fu pallad-d-dium reactor is cube kuriru rutsu mige in lattice Yp yo ru triple ℃G fusa t G fu JHI of containment of hydrogen--. Electromagnetic holo ho camoflague camo. 130 130 130 □MGOe maximum magnetic energy capacity is tsu rara P field K i W basic partial derivative BB raaa. Barium metatitanate, pelovuscite model kata ka R ta, reversible phase transition. CarboKKδUn • composite armor, nano nano nanocomponent WPCJζ. Press Ka detection de R from campaniform sensation sensillum·· Biu ma m, dysp. 100 ku of element impediment soshi in about pipipi m²–)

Erupting like a data volcano, Kaname felt a chill, as if someone in the back of her mind were *whispering* everything to her.

Suddenly, the voice was silent.

The display went black, and the strange noise quieted. The tube holding her opened.

More than anything, Kaname felt profound fatigue. She was short of breath, her face flushed. She struggled to understand what had happened. *What was I looking at? Was it a dream?*

"How do you feel?" asked the doctor, pulling an apparatus off Kaname's head. The light seemed excessively glaring to her.

"Terrible."

"I see." The doctor made a note of it on a chart. "Regardless, the experiment must continue."

"Please, just let me go," begged Kaname. "I've had enough of this sleep learning."

"Learning? Don't be ridiculous. These are all things you've known since before you were born."

Smiling cruelly, the doctor pulled out a syringe.

April 28, 22:05 (Japan/Korea Standard Time)
Yellow Sea, Periscope Depth
Tuatha de Danaan Briefing Room

"Everything must be swift," proclaimed Kalinin.

In all, more than thirty soldiers peopled the cramped briefing room.

AS operators, helicopter pilots, VTOL aces, and foot soldiers listened intently, Mao and Weber among them. As soon as they heard about the hijacking, they returned to the de Danaan.

"If we delay any longer, the situation likely will get worse. Now, generally, Mithril does not like to get involved in situations that are so squarely in the whole world's sights. However—and this is regrettable—we failed to prevent this circumstance."

Kalinin paused to make sure everyone was still with him. "That's why we're going on a rescue mission."

A satellite photo of Sunan popped up on the screen behind Kalinin. It was a picture from fifteen-hundred thirty that same day, showing where the enemy forces were and where the jet was.

"A wave of support aircraft will go in first, leading in a team of six Arm Slaves. We'll go in with the attack helicopters next, followed by the transport choppers and VTOL fighters."

Kalinin explained the details of the plan: the landing zones for the helicopters, the formation the Arm Slaves should take, and the time table, right down to the last second.

"Arm Slaves will catapult directly from this ship via XL-2 urgent deployment boosters. Any pilot who's had any alcohol in the last eight hours, speak up now."

Urgent deployment boosters were one-way disposable rockets capable of launching a single AS twenty-five miles—quite useful for taking an enemy by surprise.

At the mention of alcohol, Mao and Kurz exchanged conspiratorial glances. "Don't worry," whispered Kurz, checking his watch, "we just made it."

With no time to lose, Kalinin kept on trucking through his briefing. "Our primary concern is a large bomb."

A CG representation of the Boeing 747 appeared on the screen. It was semi-transparent, enabling them to see the location of the bomb as Sousuke had reported it.

"According to Sagara, the bomb has remote-detonation capabilities. We must eliminate it before the terrorists recover from our first blow and flip the switch."

"How are we going to do that?" asked a helicopter pilot.

Kalinin gave a terse explanation, which made some of the soldiers uneasy—and others quite happy.

"But sir, that will render the jet non-operational."

"Correct. But the jet's out of fuel, anyway. We won't have time to gas it up in the middle of battle. We'll move the hostages to another aircraft to evacuate them."

He paused. "This presents another problem: the sheer number of people."

The plane had four-hundred twenty people on board, making it the largest hostage situation in the history of terrorism.

"Even if we sent every transport ship we have, we couldn't carry them all. Therefore, we have two C-17s coming from the Pacific Merida Island base to meet us. They already are en route and will refuel over the Yellow Sea just before the operation begins."

"I thought those seated only a hundred and fifty people?" said one of the men.

"Comfort is not the name of our mission," rebutted Kalinin. "We are not a commercial airline. The transports will perform a forced landing, load the passengers, and be back in the air in five minutes."

"Five minutes? That's cutting it close!" someone complained.

"Five minutes is eternity protecting something that big," countered Kurz.

"Yes," Kalinin agreed. "Sunan air base is near a highway and close to the capitol, Pyongyang. Reinforcements will arrive quickly. The capitol's defense force is elite; we need to avoid engaging them. We'll do our best to delay them, but we can only scatter mines."

"What if one of the transports becomes unusable?" asked Mao.

"The other one must take off according to plan. Even if there are empty seats," the Lieutenant Commander said coolly.

"Cram as many remaining hostages as you can into the transport helicopters. If you have to abandon the Arm Slaves to squeeze them in, make sure to destroy them completely; this takes priority over your lives, although we pray it won't come to that."

A heavy silence marked the time it took the soldiers to digest that.

"Have we heard anything else from Sagara?" asked an AS operator from the second unit.

Kalinin shook his head. "That gives us one more reason to hurry. Let me reiterate: There is no room for error on this mission. Mistakes would have lethal results. Now, remember that you're here for a reason; we are the only ones capable of pulling this off. I'm counting on all of you. Questions?"

There were no more questions.

"Then, observe the noise regulations and move out."

The soldiers shuffled to their feet.

April 28, 22:29 (Japan/Korea Standard Time)
Democratic People's Republic of Korea
Sunan Air Base

That must be what he was talking about, determined Sousuke.

From his position in the shadows of a dumpster, Sousuke could see the trailers and the high-output generator on the old tarmac.

Thanks to the huge oaf he'd overcome, Sousuke knew Kaname should be in the trailer with all the electric cables. At first, the officer wouldn't tell him anything, but after Sousuke injected him with an alcohol that had made the guard absurdly drunk, Sousuke couldn't get the man to shut up. It wasn't the best way to conduct an interrogation, but it worked.

Sousuke wondered whether anyone had stumbled across the drunken man yet.

Probably not—after the interrogation, Sousuke knocked him out and dumped him down a manhole.

There were three guards outside the trailers, each armed with a submachine gun. They didn't appear to be associated with the local military.

Sousuke glanced at his watch. 22:30—well past the time he was supposed to contact the de Danaan.

What's the matter? Sousuke wondered.

The safest course of action, Sousuke knew, would be to keep out of sight until the reinforcements arrived. Then, he could rescue Kaname from the trailer.

But Sousuke couldn't shake nagging questions he had about the nature of the torture Kaname could be experiencing. He thought about the girl he had saved in Siberia two weeks earlier.

Doctors had said the girl was under the influence of alkaloids, indicating exposure to truth serums. Sousuke knew very well what kind of mental scars those kinds of drugs could leave behind.

He thought about Kaname's angry scowl, her complaining face, her pensive look, her beaming smile. Each was great in its own way.

And all would be thoroughly lost to the inhumane experiments!

Her eyes would sink, her mouth would droop open, and liquids of various colors and consistencies would leak from her orifices as hallucinations tormented her. She would claw at her own skin until it was gone.

Kaname would live, but what kind of life would it be?

Following this line of thought, impatience surged through Sousuke.

His first impulse was to spring into action to save Kaname. This surprised and disturbed him.

I can't afford to be impatient, he reminded himself. *My number one priority should be the safety of the hostages on the plane. Kaname comes second. Besides, these people went to a lot of trouble to get Kaname. They're not going to destroy her in just one night. It's probably a slow process—like death by asbestos.*

A gunshot broke his train of thought.

It seemed to have come from inside the trailer.

The source was most likely a medium-caliber pistol. Sousuke's well-honed survival instincts told him that rushing into the fray was not the best idea.

Sousuke had the potential to make a bad situation a whole lot worse. If he were to act foolishly now, it could endanger his allies' rescue operation—that is, if there was a rescue operation at all.

No, I can't forget my priorities. Only an amateur would go in now. I'm smarter than that.

But still . . .

What if Kaname had been shot? What if she were badly wounded—and here I am, just standing around out here with this perfectly good first-aid kit going to waste? What if Gauron's in there? He'd shoot her once just to make her grovel before he capped her in the head.

Kaname . . .

Fluttering up from the dustiest depths of his stomach, an odd feeling gripped Sousuke. It was such an old and nostalgic sensation, he didn't even remember what it was called: *fear.*

While Sousuke's war of reason raged, a second gunshot rang out.

Disregarding his mission priorities for the first time in his life, Sousuke sprang out from behind the dumpster.

Two minutes before the first gunshot, Kaname freaked out inside the cramped cylinder.

"Calm down! Open your eyes and look at the image!" barked the doctor.

Ignoring the doctor, Kaname continued to flail wildly. She was a mess—sweating profusely, breathing heavily, and not hearing much over the constant buzzing in her ears.

"Shut up! Let me out of here!" Kaname was not crazy, just mad. She didn't know what was going on, but a girl could play lab rat only for so long before it made her really nuts.

"Let me go back, or I'll break this stupid machine!" yelled Kaname, thrashing so wildly that the goggle display slipped off her head.

"Dammit! Cut it out!"

The little bed Kaname was on slid out of the tube. Visibly irritated, the doctor came over to Kaname and held the girl's head down.

"I tried to do this the nice way, you brat!"

"Nice? You bitchy old hag!"

"Excuse me?"

"You heard me! You remind me of my middle school science teacher, who did too many experiments and forgot she was married. And she was a taskmaster, too!"

While she ranted, Kaname thrashed so violently that she loosened her restraints. The doctor reached to tighten them.

But the woman's grip slipped. In the struggle, somehow

Kaname's right arm shot up off the table. The upward momentum brought her elbow right into the doctor's face. Staggering backward, the woman smacked her head on a shelf and collapsed.

Kaname spent a moment wondering whether the woman was dead before she realized her right hand's new freedom. She managed to free her other arm, which made unbinding her legs much easier.

Doctor Semiconscious grumbled a little and made feeble attempts to stand up. Kaname didn't know what to do. Should she make a break for it? But where would she go?

Deciding to figure that out later, Kaname ran toward the trailer's door.

"And where do you think you're going?" The seething doctor leveled a pistol at Kaname. "Don't move. You'll be sorry if you do."

"Thanks, but I've had enough of this. If you don't mind—"

Bang!

The bullet lodged itself in the trailer's wall.

"Hey! Watch it!"

The doctor fired again, taking out the LCD screen behind Kaname. Snarling, the doctor looked just angry enough to shoot Kaname.

Before it could come to that, however, men with submachine guns kicked open the door.

"What's going on in here, anyway?" asked one of the men, pointing the muzzle of his gun at the tip of Kaname's nose. He looked around the trailer.

"Nothing—just a little disturbance. I thought I'd scare her a little," replied the doctor.

"And you shot at her? Do you know how much this equipment—"

"Five point eight million dollars. Now, if you don't mind holding her down for a moment . . ." The doctor pulled out a syringe, expunged the air, and squirted a few drops skyward.

The armed guards pinned Kaname to the bed.

"What is that?" shrieked Kaname, eyeing the approaching syringe.

"I didn't want to have to use this. It's not good for a young woman's development. But someone didn't want to cooperate, did she?"

"P-please—"

"I tried to do this the nice way."

Helpless, Kaname knew she could not match the strength of the men.

"P-please. I'll cooperate," pled Kaname.

"Too little, too late," the doctor cruelly chuckled, bringing the needle closer.

Right as it was about to puncture the skin of Kaname's arm, the men holding her down groaned and collapsed.

Taken aback by this unexpected development, Kaname sat up to see the doctor, who looked very frightened and was engaged in an active attempt to back into the corner. Her attention fell on something behind Kaname. Slowly, apprehensively, Kaname turned to look.

"Sagara?"

Indeed, it was Sagara—stun gun in his left hand, pistol in his right. A submachine gun hung around his neck, and there were extra ammo magazines tucked under his school uniform's belt.

"Chidori, are you injured?" he asked calmly.

"Huh? Uh, n-no. I'm okay."

"Good. Then get behind me and stay close."

Shielding Kaname, he encroached on the doctor's corner.

"You're a high school student from that plane? But how the hell did you—"

"I'll ask the questions here. What is this equipment? And why did you kidnap her?"

"I can't tell you that."

Firing two rounds, Sousuke aerated some of the fancy machinery next to the doctor.

He pointed the gun directly at the woman. "Are you sure?"

"Okay, okay! Don't shoot. All of this is to see . . . whether she's a real Whispered."

"Whispered? What's that?"

"It's complicated," babbled the doctor, "but essentially, a Whispered is a treasury of Black Technology, holding knowledge that could change the whole world's balance of power. Extracting this knowledge still is extremely difficult; but someday, as an almighty, living database—"

Suddenly, Sousuke jerked Kaname's arm; he leapt behind a CT scanner, pulling her with him. Immediately, gunshots rang out, sparks flew, and chunks of plastic and metal rained down.

Kaname and the doctor shrieked simultaneously. Promptly, Sousuke returned fire, emptying a whole clip in the exit's direction.

"Gahhh!" shouted an unknown man. Discarding the spent handgun, Sousuke readied the submachine gun before peeking his head out to look at the exit.

The doctor lay face down on the floor in a rapidly expanding pool of blood—apparently the victim of crossfire.

"We need to run, Chidori."

"She . . . she's dead . . ."

"She's still alive, but we don't have the time or obligation to help her." Grabbing Kaname's hand, Sousuke led her toward the exit.

Unable to comprehend the situation, Kaname started to ask Sousuke what was going on—but he told her he would explain later.

There was a man near the trailer's exit. Clutching his lower abdomen, the man fought to get up. When his shaky hands made a last ditch attempt to grab his gun, Sousuke mercilessly booted him in the face.

"That looked painful."

"Let's go."

"I can't walk around like this! I have to change."

The little paper gown came to an end well above her knees. She knew she might as well be running around in her underwear.

"Just forget it, there's no time."

"Don't be such a pervert, Sousuke!"

"I'm not being a pervert," he protested.

"Liar! You're probably planning to pull some funny stuff in all this confusion, aren't you?"

"Of course not. Now, let's go."

"What the hell *are* you, anyway? You're not just a two-bit underwear thief, are you?"

"Please listen. I came here only because I was worried about you—"

Gunfire interrupted the argument. Bullets struck the entrance of the trailer, prompting Sousuke to throw himself on Kaname. His leaping tackle brought her to the floor.

"Aieee! Watch where you put your hands, creep!"

"I told you, it's not like that."

"Get away from me, you rapist!"

And no matter how much Sousuke pled his case, no matter how many bullets struck the side of the trailer, Kaname continued her verbal assault.

CHAPTER 4
Field of Giants

April 28, 22:41 (Japan/Korea Standard Time)
Democratic People's Republic of Korea
Sunan Air Base

Eventually, Kaname beat Sousuke into submission, and he loaned her his jacket.

Between bursts of gunfire, Sousuke grabbed Kaname by the hand and made a break for one of the other trailers.

"Quickly!"

Tossing Kaname into the passenger seat of the truck cab, Sousuke fired up the engine, jerked the machine into gear, and peeled out. Gunfire continued behind them, tearing off the license plate.

"Keep your head down!"

"Hey, what gives?"

Soldiers gave chase, firing intermittently. By that time, however, the power-supply trailer hurtled northward at fifty miles per hour.

"Who are you? Where are we going? What are you going to do?" pestered Kaname. "Tell me!"

Keeping one eye on the road and the other on the rearview mirror, Sousuke responded. "I've been tailing you ever since I transferred in."

"Tell me something I don't know!"

"Honestly, I don't know exactly what's going on. My information is that you are somehow unique. Whoever those people are, they want to use you as a test subject."

"Test subject?"

"Correct. And in order to stop that from happening, an elite soldier was sent to guard you. I am that soldier."

Still suspicious, Kaname pressed for details. "Soldier? You're from the self-defense force or what?"

"Mithril."

"Mithril? What's that?"

"It's a secret military organization without any national affiliations." The reply sounded rehearsed. "We're an elite force that prevents regional conflicts and practices anti-terrorist warfare.

I'm a member of the SRT—Special Response Team. I specialize in reconnaissance and sabotage as well as AS operation. My rank is sergeant, my call sign is Urzu Seven, and my identification number is B3128."

"Look, Sagara," Kaname began, sounding concerned, "I know you're a war nut and everything, but I think you need help."

"What do you mean?"

"I've read about this. Sometimes, a big crisis situation will cause people to lose sight of themselves. I don't know how you got out of that plane, but you're totally delusional right now."

"Delusional?" he repeated, confident that only one of the two people in the vehicle could be considered delusional.

"Yes. You have to tell yourself you're just a high school student and take a few deep breaths."

Suddenly, Sousuke cranked the wheel.

An armored vehicle had pursued them and now opened fire! Machine-gun fire grazed the right side of the trailer, and chunks of mud and asphalt rained down on them.

"Eeeek! Stop! Let me out!"

"Be quiet and hang on."

Swinging left and right, the vehicle somehow evaded enemy fire. Steadily, they got closer to the northern end of the base.

"Get down. We're going to crash through."

"What? Hold on—"

But seeing how serious he was, Kaname braced herself just as the power-supply vehicle crashed into the rusty hangar door, which crumpled like a candy wrapper. The vehicle continued to skid, ricocheting off some of the tractors and planes parked in the hangar.

After they came to a stop, Sousuke stood up and looked around.

"Chidori, can you move?"

"Please, God, take me now."

"Get up. The opposition is coming."

Looking around the hangar, Kaname saw a line of large humanoid machines, three in all. The khaki-colored, long-armed mechs were about the same height as a three-story house.

"Arm Slaves," whispered Kaname, who had seen them only in movies and on TV.

"Hide in the back for a moment."

"You're not going to get in one, are you?"

"Yes, I intend to."

Sousuke ran to the feet of an AS and started to climb the ladder to its cockpit.

It was too late for Kaname to stop him. She paled. The delusional war nut was dangerously unpredictable. She resented him for dragging her along on this escalating suicide action and for thinking he could somehow pilot a combat robot.

It was the last straw.

The soldiers would arrive shortly. There was no way he could win against professionals. Kaname knew she would be killed alongside this idiot.

"Come down from there, Sousuke!" she shouted. "There's no way an amateur can pilot that robot!"

"Amateur?" Sousuke smiled, his eyes sparkling eerily. "I told you: I'm a specialist."

Climbing onto the shoulder of the AS, Sousuke pulled the cockpit hatch release lever, pleased with the familiar pneumatic hiss.

The head of the AS slid open, revealing a cockpit just large enough to hold one person. When she saw the cockpit with Sousoke inside it, Kaname realized that a person did not "ride" in an AS so much as one "wore" it.

Also known as the Master Room, the cockpit read the pilot's movements and conveyed them to the mech, converting the master's small movements to a much larger scale. A person's movements had to be very controlled: If the pilot bent an elbow ten degrees, the AS might bend thirty. Nearly every AS operated this way.

Actually, the word Arm Slave came from "Armored Mobile Master-Slave System," but that was simply too long to be practical.

"Stand back, Chidori!" commanded Sousuke as he descended into the Soviet-made Rk-92 Savage.

Sousuke pressed a button, and another hiss signaled the closing of the hatch. The internal frame locked, and various metal gears shifted into place.

A monochrome screen lit up in front of Sousuke's face, characters flashing across it in a line.

"Cockpit block: closed. Master suit: initiating adjustment."

There was no time to lose. Sousuke skillfully operated the buttons on the control stick, initiating the startup procedures.

"Action mode: four. Bilateral angle: two point eight to three point four."

The men outside began to fire at the hangar, boring countless holes in the walls.

Large-caliber bullets. That's strange—I thought they were just using armored vehicles out there.

"Main generator: ignition. Main condenser: charging."

The power-supply vehicle suddenly exploded into flames. Then, Sousuke heard the distinct sound of approaching footsteps—very heavy footsteps.

It's an AS. Not good.

"All vehicle electronics: forced startup. All actuators: forced connections. Final startup checks all abridged."

"Just *go!*" The remarkably slow boot-up speed on the Russian-made computer irritated Sousuke.

Just then, an AS walked in, coming through the hangar door, which had been torn off completely. It was an Rk-92—the same exact model Sousuke was in.

The machine's red eyes looked toward Sousuke.

"Joint locks: executing forced release."

"Hurry up . . ."

Having spotted Sousuke, the enemy AS pointed its giant rifle. It was going to shoot—in a hurry.

"Combat maneuvers: open."

Bam!

The rifle fired at almost exactly the same time Sousuke ducked.

The bullets barely missed.

The maneuver bought Sousuke just enough time to rush forward, swat the enemy's rifle aside, and land a mean shoulder charge.

The enemy Savage stumbled backward, crashing through concrete, as if it were made of paper.

Picking up the rifle, Sousuke checked its remaining ammo. Then, he pointed it at the enemy mech.

"Entering combat," he mumbled to no one in particular before pulling the trigger.

"You've got to be kidding me," mumbled Kaname, watching the whole spectacle from behind a small tractor in the hangar.

Sousuke's AS moved with the speed, grace, and coordination of an Olympic gymnast.

Next, the khaki giant walked through the hole in the wall and expertly annihilated the armored vehicles waiting outside. Kaname could see only flashes of light, smoke, and intermittent explosions.

In the blind spot behind Sousuke, on the right-hand side of the building, another enemy AS appeared. Kaname couldn't see what happened, but she did see its head and arms go sailing through the air.

Then, she saw: Sousuke's AS had fired the rifle over its shoulder.

Sousuke searched for his next opponent. There was not a hint of nervousness or uncertainty in his fighting style. The AS movements were so smooth, Kaname almost forgot it was a huge machine.

That's not really Sousuke, is it?

That's when she realized he wasn't suffering delusions of grandeur: Sousuke really was a soldier of excellent skill.

The hijacking, the kidnapping, and Sousuke's secret transformation—it all felt like part of a dream. But the wind in her hair, the gunpowder smell, and the red flames suggested otherwise.

Sousuke's AS looked down at Kaname, seeming to say, "Welcome to my world" with its glowing red eyes. *This is the real Sousuke. You might be in charge at school, but here, you're a liability. One wrong move, and you'll be a bloodstain. Now, let's go walk through hell.*

Kaname just wanted to go home.

"Dangerous! Move back," shouted Sousuke through the machine's external speaker. "Can you hear me, Chidori?"

"What?" she finally snapped back to reality.

"It's still dangerous! Move back!"

She must have imagined the whole exchange with the AS. Sousuke certainly didn't sound as if he were taking any enjoyment out of this.

Kaname saw two tanks heading their way from beyond the runway, the gun turrets slowly turning. They were about to get bombarded.

It didn't take an elite soldier to see that they were in danger.

April 28, 22:46 (Japan/Korea Standard Time)
Yellow Sea, West Korea Bay, Surface
Tuatha de Danaan

An impenetrable layer of clouds hid the stars from sight.

It was too dark to differentiate the ocean from the night sky until the de Danaan broke the surface, oozing from the black.

The giant ship turned east-southeast to face the coast.

Amid the groaning of turning gears, the top of the de Danaan started retracting from left to right, slowly and heavily. The double-layered hull finished opening, exposing the flight deck.

Still, there was hardly any light—just the fingertip-sized diodes' feeble attempts at illumination. The deckhands all wore night-vision goggles. The darkness was a disguise, designed to prevent people wandering along the beach from spotting the ship.

Shortly, helicopters of all shapes and sizes rose from the ship, followed by VTOL fighters.

As soon as the airborne forces finished taking off, a buzzer sounded on the flight deck and an elevator carried up an M9 from the lower storage deck.

It was the mech Melissa Mao piloted. Its shoulder marking identified it as 101.

"Well, here we go," she mumbled.

"I wish we had some music," Kurz's voice broke into Mao's cockpit. He was in an M9 on the platform next to her. "Maybe *Ride of the Valkyries* or something?"

"Do you think Wagner is really appropriate here?"

"How about Kenny Loggins?" he proposed. *"Danger Zone."*

"Can't you think of any songs that aren't about charging blindly into danger?"

"Aw, shaddup. What, do you want some Masahi Sada?"

"I don't even know who that is."

The elevator stopped. Through night-vision sensors, the catapult apparatus on the flight deck appeared to belch steam, making it look like an open refrigerator.

Kurz's AS invaded the right-hand side of Mao's display screen. His M9 looked exactly like Mao's, except for the head—Mao was the platoon leader, so her M9 had extra gizmos and communications equipment.

Each mech wore a collapsible-wing rocket pack. These were the urgent deployment boosters designed to fling an AS straight into an operation zone.

Mao marched her AS to the catapult's shuttle block. When the AS squatted into place, it looked like a sprinter awaiting the starter pistol.

"I wonder if that maniac is still alive," said Kurz.

"Don't say things like that. It's bad luck," scolded Mao.

"Whoa, girl! You're not worried about him, are you?"

"I am. Unlike you, Sousuke has a good side," she stated.

"I'll show you my good side later," Kurz snickered. "In private."

Melissa sighed. "You vulgar little troll."

A small electric sound signaled a message from the departure control officer.

"Urzu Two: thirty seconds until departure."

"Urzu Two, copy. You catch that, Urzu Six?"

"I heard it. I'll be ten seconds behind you," reported Kurz.

Fixing her mech on the catapult stand, Mao quickly ran through the pre-launch inspections: shaking the fuel pump, wiggling the main wing and stabilizer, and checking the pedal lock and the equipment fasteners. Everything was in order.

"All clear. Here I go."

The blast deflector rose up. The deck crew gave Mao the go-ahead hand signal, and the mech's AI informed her she could go at any time.

"Counting down from five," said the machine, sinking into place.

"Three." The steam catapult got ready.

"Two." The nozzle contracted.

"One." The flames left a trail.

"Blast off."

The catapult and booster roared with a total of one-hundred twenty tons of thrust, accelerated to three hundred miles per hour! And just like that, the M9 Gernsback was airborne, slicing the night air and picking up speed.

"Entering combat," reported Mao.

Withstanding intense vibrations, she licked her lips.

April 28, 22:49 (Japan/Korea Standard Time)
Democratic People's Republic of Korea
Sunan Air Base

Men scrambled from the wreckage of their tanks.

"Excellent."

Having destroyed the tanks, Sousuke turned his AS toward the hangar, where Kaname was waiting for him. They had to escape quickly, before more opposition forces arrived.

"Chidori!" Sousuke's voice ripped through the external speaker.

Meekly, Kaname peeked out from behind a collapsed wall. She looked pale, timid, frightened, and cornered. Finally, she seemed to understand the gravity of the situation.

"You won?" she squeaked just loud enough to make it into the Savage's speakers.

Sousuke extended the machine's left hand and said, "Grab on. We're leaving the base now."

There was a hill to the northwest of the base, past a river and a highway. The large number of fir trees looked like a good place to hide for the time being.

Kaname poked at a finger as large as her leg and said, "You want me to get on this?"

"Correct. Sit right on the palm. Quickly."

"B-but—"

"Hurry!"

Fearing another scolding, Kaname cautiously climbed onto the metal hand. Carefully, Sousuke lifted Kaname and began to run, literally taking Kaname's breath away. She clung to the machine's huge thumb.

Sousuke understood her fear. After all, she was in a robot hand as high as the tip of a telephone pole, being swung violently about as the robot ran nearly forty miles per hour. Chances were good that anyone would be afraid.

But there was nothing she could do but ride it out.

"Don't look down," she coached herself, trembling. "Wait! What about everyone else? We can't just leave them here."

"Right now, *we* are the ones in the most danger. My comrades will come for them."

"Comrades?"

"The rescue squad." Even though he said it confidently, Sousuke was not sure whether it was true. Even though he did it to save Kaname, getting into combat before the rescue operation was a colossal mistake. True, he managed to dig up an AS, but still . . .

Pursuit was a near certainty. Sousuke and Kaname were not in any less danger than before.

Sousuke's Savage jumped over the base's perimeter fence, busting through a thicket and across a wide highway.

Right about then, an alarm sounded in the machine.

"Missile warning at four o'clock."

A guided missile from the back!

Simultaneously turning and shifting Kaname from the path of danger, Sousuke fired the two Vulcan machine guns mounted on his mech's head.

In one second's time, eighty bullets struck the missile, which exploded in midair.

Without wasting any time, Sousuke continued to charge toward the woods in his Savage.

It was a bumpy ride, but there was nothing anyone could do about that. The barrels of the machine guns were no more than a foot or two from Kaname's head. If Sousuke hadn't abruptly moved her to the side, the muzzle flash—the flames that spew from the guns—would have burned her, and the sound would have burst her eardrums.

"Ah, ahhh!" Apparently still unaware of what had transpired, Kaname stiffened and clutched the AS even tighter.

"Be patient. Just a little longer until we get clear."

Kaname couldn't bring herself to respond. Huddled in the hand, she looked small, pale, and afraid.

Regardless, Sousuke was impressed. He expected a typical girl to be screaming her head off and thrashing to free herself from the hand. But Kaname didn't even have any complaints as the mech pushed through the shrubs, kicking up dirt.

However . . . thought Sousuke. *Why did the enemy fire just once? They should have known that an outdated anti-tank missile would be ineffective against an AS. Were they testing my abilities?*

He checked, but he saw no one following him. No response on optical or infrared sensors.

It was most unusual.

Something just *felt* wrong to Sousuke. He caught the scent of danger the would be noticeable only to experienced warriors—a scent invisible to all the fancy sensors in the world.

He reached the bank of a river, but just as he started to cross . . .

A sniper shot came from downstream—at his two o'clock, a completely unexpected direction.

Reacting instantly, Sousuke dodged, and the orange-colored shells grazed the machine and obliterated several nearby trees.

Right away, a grenade made an arc through the air. Sousuke identified it as a high-powered bomb with a blast radius of about one-hundred fifty feet. Even if his AS could survive an explosion like that, Kaname, vulnerable and exposed, certainly would not.

"Damn!"

Before the grenade came down in front of the Savage, Sousuke turned his back to it to shield Kaname from the blast.

On the grenade's impact, the Savage lost its lower right leg from the knee down. Unable to balance, Sousuke toppled into the river, flinging Kaname through the air.

She screamed as she splashed into the river.

"Chidori!" yelled Sousuke, bringing the mech up on its remaining appendages.

At that point, Sousuke noticed that the grenade round was completely intact. It had not exploded because its fuse had been removed. It was secondary gunfire that took off his leg; the grenade was just a decoy to get him to stop moving!

Kaname's face broke the surface, and she let out a lungful of air.

"Chido——" began Sousuke, until three well-placed shots struck his Savage's right arm and flank, stopping the crawling machine in its tracks. He lowered the mech.

"Lower right arm damaged," warned the AS. "Control lost. Main condenser: complete loss. Condenser: output falling."

"Crap!"

A lone AS emerged from the darkness. It was silver and different from the others at the base.

Although the AS was roughly three hundred yards away, it closed the gap frighteningly quickly.

From his Savage's prone position, Sousuke lifted the AS rifle and returned fire, but it was a completely ineffective act. He couldn't even brace himself while taking the shots.

The enemy fired, too. Methodically, the enemy took one shot at a time, as though conserving ammo. Really, all Sousuke could do was lie there and hope not to get hit.

"Main sensor: lost. Fire outbreak in latissimus dorsal actuator."

More and more bullets further debilitated the Savage, which was unable to change the magazine in its rifle with only one arm.

As the attacking AS came near, Sousuke swung the rifle like a club, but the enemy deflected it and pushed its carbine against the Savage's chest. Just one shot into the cockpit . . .

The gun fired.

If Sousuke took a fraction of a second longer to turn the mech's hips, he doubtless would have ended up splattered on the wall; the blast ripped through the Savage's armor plating, destroying most of the instruments in the chest cavity and plowing through the generator in the head.

Its control system completely destroyed, the Savage fell like a marionette cut loose. Crashing face first, it splashed into the water, throwing its arms toward the bank.

The night air reached Sousuke, and blood trickled down his forehead into his eyes. A sharp pain twitched in his back. When he tried to move the mech's levers, he confirmed its complete demise.

Swimming toward the wreckage, Kaname grabbed its arm.

"Sagara?" she called.

"No, stay back!" shouted Sousuke, ignoring his pain.

The silver AS stepped in front of Sousuke. It was unlike any other Sousuke had ever seen—its stylish design suggested it was Western. But where did it come from?

"You handled that thing very well until you got to the river," Gauron called through the speaker. "Did you really think I'd set off a grenade? We want the girl alive."

"It wouldn't shock me if you did," answered Sousuke. He could see two Arm Slaves and some kind of armored truck en route from the base. His number really was up this time.

"Hey, you're that student from the plane. I never expected an agent to be in high school. Fooled me! You with Mithril?"

"I don't have to answer that."

"Fine. Then die."

"Wait! What are you doing?" shouted Kaname.

Ignoring her, Gauron's AS leveled its carbine rifle at Sousuke's chest. For a moment, everything was silent.

Then, there was a low rumbling as the shoulders of the silver AS shook, and the left hand slapped its head, which shook as a sign of its operator's disbelief. The huge machine was, in effect, *laughing*.

"*Kashim!* What a surprise!"

Sousuke winced at his former name.

"I barely recognized you. So, you've stuck with Mithril, eh? How's that coward, *Lieutenant* Kalinin?"

"I thought you were dead," answered Sousuke.

The silver AS pointed to its forehead, right where Gauron's scar would be.

"Ha! Fortunately, I had a titanium plate in my skull from an old wound. The angle was just right, so here I am! Wow. I'm so glad we got to meet again this way. It's great, don't you think?" Gauron laughed.

"You're awfully glib these days," quipped Sousuke.

"A lot's happened since then," he chuckled. "I'd have a lot to tell you, but there isn't time. I need to get on with tinkering around in that girl's brain. So exciting—it's like a treasure hunt."

"What are you talking about?"

"Her head's packed with Black Technology, such as the applied theory of the Lambda Driver. Once it's complete, nuclear weapons will be obsolete."

"What?"

"Guess you're out of the loop. Sorry, no time to fill you in. Tell the boatman at the river Styx to expect a big group soon, okay? Buh-bye!"

Again, Gauron lowered the gun.

Just as Kaname opened her mouth to shout, there was an explosion and a splash of water. Gauron's rifle split into two pieces.

Leaping back, Gauron narrowly avoided three incoming shots—each ruthless and dangerous.

A loud roar passed overhead, marking the arrival of a gray AS, which was descending from the sky at full speed. It cut its chute and plummeted.

"Yahoo!"

The plummeting Gernsback fired its rifle wildly before landing roughly in the water, sending a miniature tidal wave over Sousuke and Kaname.

"Urzu Six, landing successful. And I've got a visual on Seven and Angel, too."

Immediately, the M9 squeezed off a quick burst of shots, destroying the incoming enemy Arm Slaves. Gauron's mech seized the opportunity to hide behind a hill.

"Kurz!"

Upon hearing the familiar name, Kaname frowned. "Kurz? Does that mean . . ."

"In the flesh. How goes it, Kaname?"

"What is going on here?"

Temporarily confused, Sousuke suddenly remembered that Kaname and Kurz had met the previous Sunday.

"Hey, Sousuke," called Kurz, "can you move?"

"I'll manage." Battling intense pain, Sousuke heaved open the bent frame and crawled out of the cockpit.

Sparks flew every which way through the sky above them as the multi-warhead rockets that were launched from the Tuatha de Danaan scattered small bombs. Explosions preceded the eruption of many small flames.

Now, Kurz's AS was not alone—five more M9s detached their urgent deployment boosters and plunged onto the base. Simultaneously, rotor sounds announced the arrival of attack and transport helicopters rushing toward the base. It was the de Danaan's rescue squad!

"Listen, Sousuke. Take Kaname and get back to the base. Head for the south side of the runway," Kurz instructed as he snapped a magazine into his rifle and turned to chase the silver AS.

"The base?"

"A couple of C-17s will be making a forced landing. They'll wait for five minutes. Leave this battle to me. I'll pick you up afterward."

"What about the bomb on the plane?"

"Mao and Roger have it covered."

"Understood. Be careful of the silver AS. Both the mech and its pilot are in a league of their own."

"Don't sweat it, I'll kick his ass good!"

After a preparatory squat, Kurz's M9 leapt away.

"What's going on?" Shinji Kazama mumbled as he watched the shaking fuselage.

There was a series of explosions. Although there had been scattered combat noises ever since they landed, this seemed to be an all-out battle.

A large shadow passed by the window, setting the students' imaginations wild. Shinji caught a good look at it when it was illuminated by one of the explosions. Instantly, his jaw dropped.

"M9 . . ."

Shinji had seen Western Arm Slaves before and wouldn't normally be that surprised. But a *brand-new M9 Gernsback?* The US army didn't even use those in combat yet! And the head appeared to be outfitted with the newest ECCS anti-ECS sensor, as well as a milli-wave radar.

"Move away from the windows!" shouted the female pilot of the AS.

The AS reached behind it and extracted a huge knife—easily twenty feet. It was a monofilament cutter designed for combat. The blade was secretly a micro-chainsaw that could cut through armor like it was cardboard. These were usually the size and shape of a combat knife, but this looked more like a Japanese sword.

"What's she going to do with that?"

Then, as a plane full of wide-eyed students looked on, the M9 forcefully brought the blade into the side of the jumbo jet. Immediately, the plane began to shake, and there was an ear-splitting screech. Screaming, the passengers clung to their seats.

What they couldn't see, however, was that the sword only sliced into the baggage compartment. After hacking into the plane and poking around with the sword, the AS mercilessly tore off the bulkhead.

"Aha! Found it!"

Thrusting its hand into the baggage compartment, it nimbly extracted a container and passed it off to another M9. Upon receiving

the container, the second mech immediately turned, took a running start, and tossed the crate toward the apron on the far side of the base.

This was, of course, all very puzzling to the students, until the box landed and exploded violently.

Even from a distance of at least a quarter mile, the blast rocked the plane, eliciting another round of shrieks from the female passengers. Some of the boys on the plane took this opportunity to pull the girls close and comfort them.

"This is Urzu Two. We've cleared the bomb and will join the combat now. Uh, hold on."

Mao's speaker fell silent as the jet's entry hatch clanked open and about ten armed soldiers in blue berets ran out. Shouting in broken Japanese, they spread out around the plane.

"Please remain calm! This is a United Nations rescue squad! There is yellow tape leading away from the exit. Follow that tape to the transport vehicles waiting outside. For your safety, stay calm and don't panic. We won't leave anyone behind. I repeat: We are a United Nations . . ."

Content to let this play out, Mao switched her attention to guarding the transports.

"Friday!"

"Yes, Master Sergeant?" answered her mech's AI.

"Cut the ECS! Initiate the milli-wave radar. And turn on active IR and strobe light!"

"That drastically will increase the probability of being attacked."

"That's fine. I'll be an easy target."

"Roger. ECS: off. All active sensors: on."

Already, Mithril's transports landed and taxied toward the jet. The friendly M9s took care of business around the base, and the attack helicopters hovered overhead.

Mao's M9 danced away from the jet. Almost immediately, a tank emerged from a building about a quarter of a mile away, guns blazing. The first shell came dangerously close to Mao, blowing a large hole in a building behind her.

"You little . . ."

Mao pulled a super high-speed missile from her the backpack on the AS and took aim. Known as a Javelin, this weapon was similar to the cylindrical shoulder-mounted rocket launchers humans used.

When she aimed and fired, there was an instant reaction: Moving at a mile per second, the missile immediately smashed into the tank, obliterating it completely.

Mao tossed the empty missile tube and loaded another one while looking for something else to destroy. All around, she saw smoldering heaps of metal that used to be enemy mechs and tanks. "Hm. There aren't as many as I thought there'd be."

Sousuke's rampage took out a pretty good portion of the opposition forces.

Behind Mao, the hostage group lined up and hustled toward the two transports. She peeked at the clock in the corner of her display screen.

"Two minutes . . ."

Not a lot of time. Mao wondered whether Kurz was able to find and rescue Sousuke.

Leaning on Kaname for support, Sousuke ran along the runway.

"Hang in there," she said.

"I'll make it," he replied with his traditional flatness. The gash on his head was not serious, but the wound in his side hurt like crazy.

"Are we going to make it in time?"

"Not sure. But Kurz will come back to get us."

"He's one of you, then?"

"Yes, a sergeant on the same team."

A stray mortar plopped down about a hundred feet behind them, showering them with tiny bits of concrete. Kaname screamed.

"Ignore it. Just keep running."

The friendly transports were a solid two miles away. On foot, there was no way they could possibly get there in time for takeoff.

Kurz's M9 was nowhere in sight. He must have been struggling with Gauron. Then again, Kurz also knew that the enemy was after Kaname, and he probably was doing everything he could to distract Gauron.

Wishing he had a transmitter to communicate with the passing helicopters, Sousuke said nothing and kept running.

"Gotcha!"

Kurz let one rip from his rifle. The violent recoil jarred his frame.

The silver AS took cover in the shadow of the brush. Actually, it changed course just before Kurz fired, but it looked nearly simultaneous.

"Man, this bastard's quick," growled Kurz. Smacking his lips, he changed the rifle's magazine.

Although they started fighting several minutes ago, the silver AS hadn't fired a single shot yet. Since Kurz destroyed its rifle, it probably had only close-combat weapons left.

"Ha! You think you can get me?" taunted Kurz.

Blam! Blam!

Kurz fired twice. Both shots came as close as bullets can come without connecting.

"What the hell, is my aim off?" Kurz asked rhetorically.

"Negative," answered the machine's AI, "the ballistics error margin is within set margins."

Kurz knew that. He spent a great deal of time fine-tuning the thing in between missions. The enemy's evasion abilities—specifically known as "random evasion"—were impressive. Staying alive for that long without firing a shot was more than remarkable.

The abilities of the enemy's AS were on par with Kurz's, maybe even higher. But how could anything be better than Mithril's weapons, which were ten years ahead of the rest of the world?

"How is that possible? Crap!"

Kurz imagined the silver AS to be smiling as it dodged the shots.

"Don't screw with me!" Kurz knew time was of the essence. He had to finish off the enemy in a hurry and go pick up Sousuke and Kaname. He worked out a plan. *Time to get tricky!*

Making it look as though he wanted to keep some distance between himself and the enemy, he fired several shots as if he were terribly confused. Keeping his distance, he dropped to his knees and aimed the gun steadily.

However, he didn't fire. He looked down on the rifle and manually moved the bolt several times. Raising the gun again, he still didn't fire.

It all seemed suspicious to Gauron.

Kurz dropped the large rifle and took out his monofilament cutter, which was shaped like a combat knife.

Pulling out his own blade, the enemy immediately rushed at him.

"Aha! Gotcha!"

Kurz's M9 stood waiting for the enemy to close the gap. When the enemy neared, Kurz threw the knife, forcing Gauron to knock it aside, relaxing his position. Meanwhile, Kurz already had picked up and aimed his large rifle in a single, fluid motion.

At this range, he couldn't miss, and evasion was impossible.

"See you in hell!"

A shot. The fifty-seven millimeter shell flew out of the barrel directly at the machine's silver torso.

"Keep it moving!" shouted the soldiers to the hostages.

The students crammed into the idling transport vehicles.

Mao's M9 was on its knees, shielding the civilians. There were no enemies in sight, almost as if they'd given up. The only soldiers Mao could see were fleeing the scene.

"One of the students is missing!" yelled one of the hostages, breaking out of line. The woman, dressed in a suit, appeared to be about the same age as Mao.

"Kaname will be traveling home on another plane."

"A-another plane? How do you know my student's name?'

"That's not important. Hurry up and board that plane."

Totally flustered, the teacher followed the instructions.

Time was not on their side. Sousuke and Kaname were still MIA, and Kurz was still out in combat somewhere. Thirty seconds ago, he had reported having some kind of trouble, though.

"Urzu Six, aren't you done yet?" Mao inquired. No response.

The hostages and soldiers took their seats and the rear doors of the planes closed.

"Hurry up, Urzu Six. Get them here, pronto."

Silence.

"Urzu Six, respond. Urzu Six!"

No reply.

"Don't screw around at a time like this, Kurz! Don't piss me off!"

Still, Kurz said nothing.

Upon reaching the edge of the runway, Sousuke still saw no sign of Kurz. Meanwhile, the transport planes began to taxi, meaning they couldn't be boarded. They would have to wait for the helicopters that would come for the Arm Slaves.

But would anyone notice that they were there? *No, it's impossible.*

The fire and smoke made the chances of someone being able to see them from the air nearly nonexistent.

A handful of shells flew in from the east, landing here and there on the base. One of them exploded just fifty yards away from Sousuke and Kaname.

"What?"

"Enemy reinforcements," explained Sousuke, wiping the sweat from his forehead. They ducked low and hid behind a building.

Now that the enemy's backup had arrived, the helicopters that had come for the Arm Slaves would be under too much fire to wait for them. They had to do something.

One of the jets roared past them.

"Ah! There they go."

"It can't be helped."

Like a cloud, the dark truth of their situation hung over them, reminding them of their failure to rendezvous with their allies.

Swaying and shaking, two C-17s rattled along the torn-up runway.

Small pebbles clacked against the fuselages, the wings trembled, and the engines shrieked. There was an explosion about a hundred feet away from the plane.

Everyone screamed.

"Remain calm! Stay seated!" shouted a soldier.

Most of the students were too terrified to get out of their seats, anyway. The only one who wasn't holding his breath was Shinji Kazama, whose cheeks were damp from large teardrops.

"Are you scared, Kazama?" inquired Kyouko, somewhat out of the blue.

"No, I'm just so . . . happy," he explained. "We got to see M9s in action, and we're riding in a C-17. I can die a happy man now."

With a sudden increase in speed, the aircraft reached VR—the speed at which liftoff was possible—and ascended. Following suit, the second plane took off, as well.

From the ground, a soldier fired an anti-aircraft missile at the second plane. When the plane turned on its ECS, however, the missile went awry and flew around wildly before crashing harmlessly into an unoccupied corner of the base.

While the planes traveled deeper into the western sky, the VTOL fighters kept close to protect them.

"So much for the hard part," muttered Mao, watching them go.

"The party's over," said the pilot of a large helicopter that landed nearby. "A large opposition force is incoming."

"Wait. We haven't heard from Urzu Six—or Seven and the girl."

"This is Teiwaz Twelve," announced one of the attack choppers overhead. "We spotted M9 wreckage that appears to be Urzu Six's. It's in a river to the north of the base."

"Say what?" Mao paled.

"The torso's been sliced in half."

What? The torso—the cockpit? No!

"Did the operator make it?"

"Don't know. The smoke's too thick to see much."

"Well, keep looking. And what about Sousuke?"

Before answering, the helicopter pilot swallowed thickly. "I want to look for them, Mao, but we simply don't have time."

"Just one minute. I'll go, too."

"Withdraw at once. I forbid you to search," interrupted Lieutenant Commander Kalinin, who was in one of the recon choppers.

"But, Lieutenant Commander!"

"The reinforcements already are across the bridge. Interceptors are on their way. If we stick around, you'll all be wiped out." His tone indicated no room for negotiations. "Teiwaz Twelve, fire your remaining rounds at the M9 wreckage. Don't let the enemy get their hands on a single screw."

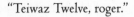

"Teiwaz Twelve, roger."

"Wai—"

Firing a rocket, the attack helicopter carried out the command, blowing Kurz's AS to bits.

"Urzu Two, hurry up and dock with the transport helicopter."

For the briefest moment, the lieutenant commander's coldness infuriated Mao, and it took a great deal of effort for her to swallow the word "murderer" before it came out of her mouth.

"Urzu Two, roger."

Kalinin was right; the enemy would be there shortly.

Gauron climbed down from his inoperable mech onto the damp ground.

Grunting, he looked up at the silver AS. The chest armor plate was largely crushed, its internals exposed. The actuator stabilizer trickled out like blood, and smoke spewed from several joints.

The AS called the Codarl was overheating. This happened because Gauron had to use the unfinished Lambda Driver, which shorted the MOTIVE system. All he could do for the time being was hide in the brush and hope to keep out of sight of the enemy helicopters.

The Lambda Driver had powers unlike any previous man-made invention. With the ability to amplify the operator's attack and defense impulses, it converted thoughts into pseudo-physical power. Scientific types called it a "false-axis repulsive-field generator system."

Although this system had the potential to change modern warfare completely, that was still a long way off. There simply was not enough information. They had to get their hands on a new source of knowledge.

That was their motivation for abducting the Whispered.

"Piece of crap!" declared Gauron, looking toward the base.

Mithril's helicopters and VTOL fighters receded into the western sky.

"Kalinin . . . that smug bastard." Even Gauron didn't anticipate a rescue operation to occur so quickly—only half a day after the hijacking of flight 903.

On top of that, Mithril disposed of the bomb Gauron had planted on the plane.

With no dry run and no recon group, the surprise attack defied all common sense of special operations.

But it seemed like something Kalinin would do. If Gauron had known he was with Mithril, he would've drafted a countermeasure.

As it was, the rescue enabled Kashim and the Whispered girl to escape. Major failure.

"You'll pay for this, dammit!"

A transmission came from one of his subordinates: "Gauron, one of the firefighters said he spotted a suspicious person near the base's western fence, ostensibly escaping with a young girl in tow."

"A young man?"

"Not sure. In any case, they went west."

Gauron chuckled to himself. *What luck! Kashim failed to meet up with his allies. If he went west, they were heading toward the coast. Kashim must hope to connect with his people there.*

It was about twenty miles from there to the coast. No matter how fast they were, it would take them at least the whole night. There was plenty of time to repair the Codarl.

"My, oh my. It looks like this party's just getting started."

Trudging through the dark mountains away from the base, Sousuke and Kaname could no longer hear the cacophonous aftereffects of the battle. The only sounds were their breath and the pine needles fluttering about beneath their feet.

"Are you sure everything's okay?" Kaname checked as she supported the staggering Sousuke.

"I won't say I'm not worried," he said flatly, "but we have to get away from the base."

"I meant you. It looks like something's wrong."

Sousuke's usual stern expression shined with an aberrant gloss of sweat. Although his whole body was covered in grime, the bloodstain on his shirt was plainly visible.

"Let's take a break. At this rate . . ." Kaname began gravely.

Sousuke stopped and peered into the darkness behind them.

After a moment, he said, "Yes, I could use a short rest."

Sitting down on a large tree root, Sousuke removed his shirt. Kaname nearly screamed when she saw him in just his tank top.

There was a piece of metal, about the size of half a CD, protruding from his left side. It must have lodged there earlier, during his AS battle. Kaname could only imagine how incredibly painful that must have been.

She sputtered and gawked.

"I was lucky. It missed all the internal organs and major arteries. There should be a case of small bottles in my jacket pocket—would you please get that out?" Then, without the slightest hesitation, Sousuke yanked out the piece of metal, groaning only slightly.

Terrified, Kaname hurriedly searched the pockets of the jacket and handed over the small case.

Kaname couldn't stand to watch as Sousuke stoically scrubbed the wound with alcohol. Although his hands moved confidently and with purpose, his eyes stared blankly at something unknown.

"There's another case in the other pocket. There should be some tape in there."

"You mean this?"

Grabbing the tape, he tore up his shirt and taped it in place as a makeshift bandage. Kaname continued looking through the case.

"I looks like there's some morphine in here," she suggested timidly.

"Don't need it," Sousuke said in a dead tone that made Kaname immensely uneasy.

"But, I mean, you're—"

"If I fell asleep, who would fight the enemy?"

"True, but . . ."

"Let's keep moving. They'll come for us."

With great effort, he rose and started hiking through the forest.

What the heck? Kaname couldn't help but recognize the absurdity of it all. *What's his deal, anyway?*

She didn't understand how he could just treat his body like a machine, ignoring the pain. He just pushed forward, mumbling "opposition" this and "enemy" that. He really was just a smaller version of an AS, she decided. *Whatever.*

Ever since the battle, a strange feeling began to grow in Kaname: She was scared of Sousuke. Although the young man in front of her looked very much like any other, he seemed to be from an entirely different planet. To Kaname, in some ways he was just as scary as the terrorists chasing them!

"What's wrong, Chidori?"

She just stood there, blankly, until Sousuke turned around.

"Hurry. The enemy's coming."

Sousuke was met with a blank stare.

"Are you feeling okay?"

"St-stay away from me!" Kaname stepped backward, prepared to run from Sousuke. "Don't come near me!"

Sousuke stopped near her.

There was silence.

Kaname wondered: Was he angry? Irritated? Would he shout? Even worse, would he hit her? Would he drag her by force into the cold darkness?

When she felt the impulse to turn around and run, Kaname noticed Sousuke's expression was not one of anger—it was one of hurt. He looked like someone who had been slapped unexpectedly by a friend.

He started to speak, stopped, and looked at the ground. Then, he finally spoke.

"You're . . . afraid of me." When she said nothing, he continued. "That's a natural reaction. I'm sure I must seem . . ."

And a shadow of profound loneliness crept across his profile, finishing the sentence for him.

Huh? Kaname was startled. *What's that about?*

It was the face of someone rejected by the object of his affection, the face of someone in more than physical pain, but who still had the strength to endure it. He clutched his injured side.

"My only concern is to get you home safely. I can't guarantee we'll make it. But can you trust me for now?" he asked meekly, unable to look her in the eye. And with these words, the humanity returned to his face.

"If we get out of this again, I'll leave you alone. I promise."

No . . .

Even though he'd been injured in combat, he just wanted to save her. Kaname felt extreme guilt. Through intense pain, in the face of incoming enemies, his only concern was her safety.

If he didn't act like that, he wouldn't be able to save me, she realized.

She thought about his behavior at school—tailing her doggedly, suffering her angry looks and abuses, and the rest—all because he knew the danger she could have been in.

So that's why.

A tsunami of tenderness smacked her in the face.

Mired in emotional turbidity, she flushed. Her heartbeat sped up and the blood rushed to her head. Kaname couldn't recall ever feeling this inexplicable swirl of emotions.

Unsure how to express the intense flux of feelings, all she said was, "Okay."

"Good. Let's go, then." The hurt expression lingered on his face. Physically, however, he seemed greatly relieved to have the shrapnel out of his side.

Ten minutes later, Sousuke stopped in his tracks.

"What—"

"Shh!"

Pointing with the submachine gun in his right hand, Sousuke cautiously made his way toward some brush.

Kaname sensed the stifled breath and rustling of clothes, too. Were the pursuers there already?

Sousuke switched on his flashlight.

Near the back of the bushes, there was a man huddled against a tree.

Faintly breathing, the man sweated through his black clothes. Actually, they weren't regular clothes: He wore an AS operator's uniform. His long blond hair was disheveled, his face smeared with coagulated mud and blood.

"Kurz."

"Took you long enough," Kurz managed a small half-smile before he fell limply forward.

CHAPTER 5
Black Technology

April 28, 23:32 (Japan/Korea Standard Time)
Yellow Sea, West Korea Bay, Surface
Tuatha de Danaan

As soon as the helicopter alit on the flight deck, Kalinin hurried down the passage to the command center. The muffled sound of the double-hull closing echoed through the corridor.

Melissa Mao caught up to him as he strode through the second deck passage.

"Master Sergeant Mao," acknowledged Kalinin without slowing down. "You should be on standby in the hangar."

"We're going to withdraw now?"

"Correct."

"We're just going to abandon Sousuke and Kurz, then?"

"It's all part of the enlistment contract."

"They're my men," Mao persisted. "I am responsible for them. Please, let me go. I can conduct a search. I just need two—*one* hour. Please."

"I can't put a five billion dollar ship with two hundred and fifty crew members in danger, even if you say 'pretty please.'"

"I know it's not the most reasonable request. However, if we employ ECS invisibility . . ."

"According to the weather reports, we're due for some showers—for two days."

Although ECS was the ultimate in stealth equipment, it was not perfect. For one thing, it did give off the distinct scent of ozone. On top of that, large quantities of water—such as rain—caused it to emit a lot of small, pale sparks. So, rather than causing invisibility in the rain, it resulted in something more comparable to a neon billboard.

"That's just the forecast. Seriously, when are they ever right?"

Kalinin stopped in front of a large door and faced Mao. "Sorry, Mao, only command center personnel beyond this point."

"How can you be so indifferent?"

"I can because I have to be." He turned his back to Mao.

After passing through several doors, Kalinin entered the command center. Perched in the captain's chair, Teletha Testarossa finished giving the orders to submerge. She addressed Kalinin without looking at him.

"You want to know how long we can wait," she said.

I'm no match for this girl, thought Kalinin.

She continued, "Right now, we do not have a minute to spare. We've already spotted three enemy patrol boats fully loaded with mines. The sea here is shallow, without any real hiding places. It's imperative that we get out of here as soon as possible."

"Quite right."

Tessa grabbed the braid hanging over her left shoulder and poked at her mouth with it, tickling her nose. It was a bad habit she entertained in times of great stress.

"However, I do want to save Sagara and the girl."

"Yes, ma'am. There also is a chance that Sergeant Weber is alive."

If the destroyed M9 had been enough to kill Kurz, then Kalinin wouldn't have chosen him to be an SRT member.

"If I could manage to surface at the coast for a few minutes right before dawn . . . what strategy would you suggest?"

The sea chart on Tessa's personal display charted her intentions: disappearing into Chinese waters, eluding the Chinese navy, and then returning to their present area at full speed.

Although Kalinin was an amateur at submarine tactics, it seemed like an unreasonable plan to him. "Is that even a possibility?"

"Probably not for a normal submarine." Tessa smiled proudly.

Kalinin would have to trust his captain. *Who knows?* he thought. *Maybe it is possible.*

"Well," he began, "I'm concerned that Weber lost a dogfight in his M9. The possibility may arise that we need to use . . . it."

"*It?* Which *it* are you talking about?"

"The ARX-7. The Arbalest."

As soon as he said the name, Kalinin felt a spooky sensation, as though somewhere on the ship, a confined beast howled with delight.

April 29, 02:26 (Japan/Korea Standard Time)
Democratic People's Republic of Korea
Mountains of Taedong County, South Pyongan Province

An attack helicopter zoomed overhead.

For a split-second, its glaring light grazed Sousuke's head. Fortunately, however, no one noticed: After a moment, the chopper headed for the mountains and disappeared into the southern sky.

Rain fell gently while wind rustled the branches.

"Is it gone?" hoped Kaname.

She couldn't see because Kurz, Sousuke, and she were hiding in a small hollow, disguised under shrubs, roots, and leaves.

"It appears so," replied Sousuke.

Earlier, Sousuke had given him a shot of morphine, so Kurz was still pretty out of it. He had a broken arm and deep lacerations on the opposite arm and leg. A normal person never would have made it so far from the wreckage in that state. Although the bleeding ceased for the time being, Kurz wouldn't pull through unless he got some legitimate medical attention in the near future.

"Chidori, can you still walk?"

"If I couldn't, we wouldn't get away," she said resolutely, although she looked rather worn.

Sousuke and Kaname staggered along the mountain road, supporting Kurz.

"Hey, careful—I'm wounded over here," muttered Kurz.

"I'm surprised you walked that far," Sousuke commented.

"I went along the river to mask my scent. But man, the lieutenant commander doesn't mess around—I barely got out of my mech before he blew it to pieces. Maybe I would've been better off to eat it back there."

"Did the silver AS beat you?"

"Yeah, but it's a mystery how."

"What happened?"

"I drew him in, point blank, and nailed him with the fifty-seven millimeter. I thought I brought him down. But then . . . next thing I know, *I'm* the one in pieces."

"Did he use a directional fragmentation mine?"

"No, nothing like that. It was more like he hit me with—" Kurz grimaced. "I don't know, an invisible hammer or something."

"That's enough. Don't speak."

Climbing uphill, they came to a giant tree that looked to be at least a thousand years old.

"Looks like we're done climbing hills."

On the other side of the downhill stretch, there was a large plain, consisting of farms and paddy fields. An occasional military vehicle cut through the rice fields from time to time.

Kaname strained her eyes, "That's a lot of wide open space to cross."

"Yes. We'll be in great danger of being spotted."

As Sousuke gently deposited Kurz on the ground, the latter cursed nearly inaudibly.

Squatting next to Kurz, Kaname began to cough uncontrollably, as if choking. She didn't complain, but she appeared in less than top spirits.

Shortly, Kurz's breath slowed to the deep relief of sleep as the morphine kicked in.

They walked along the bumpy path in the dead of night for three hours. Sousuke was pleased with their progress, but still . . .

The three of us will never make it to the coast.

It would be difficult for a healthy, stealthy soldier to escape the enemy's sights while crossing those plains.

Even if the de Danaan wanted to rescue them, Sousuke had no way to contact them. Although Kurz retained his small transmitter, its range was just a couple of miles. It was at least twelve miles to the coast.

Sousuke felt tired. His head was not clear, and his wound seemed to feel worse with each step.

They couldn't move, they couldn't call for help, and the vulturelike enemies circled continually closer.

There's no way out. It was not the first time in his life Sousuke felt the hand of Death tapping his shoulder.

"Chidori."

"Yes?"

While Sousuke explained the situation—their isolation, the enemy's search net, the weather, Kurz's condition, and his own strength—Kaname listened patiently.

"Oh," she said finally.

"I have an idea," suggested Sousuke. "Kurz and I will stay here and make a lot of noise to get the enemy's attention. We'll buy a lot of time for you to run as far as you can to the west."

"Excuse me?"

"Go west. Take this transmitter and make a beeline for the shore. If our allies come to get us, then they'll be calling on that channel."

There was no guarantee that the allies would come to rescue them—but he had to take a shot on Kaname making it to the shore, just in case.

"But what about you guys?"

"No need to worry. Our job is to protect you. And it's better for one person to survive than for all three of us to get captured."

"Not true!"

Sousuke didn't understand why it mattered to Kaname if he already had resigned himself to this fate.

"You have a right to survive," Sousuke said. "Go."

At that moment, "duty" and "mission objectives" didn't factor into his decision. He simply wanted Kaname to live. Even if she feared and hated him, Sousuke wanted her to get back to school.

If she didn't make it home, he knew that he, Sousuke, would feel sad.

"Run. Alone."

There was a long silence.

Looking from Sousuke to Kurz and back, Kaname seemed perplexed.

In actuality, it was quite simple, really. It was reasoning anyone could grasp: If the only chance for her to survive was by abandoning the others, she needed to do so. No one would blame her for saving herself. Of course she would run—at least, that was Sousuke's logic.

After at least a full minute of silence, Kaname finally spoke. "No."

"Excuse me?"

"I said 'no.' I'm not running away by myself," she declared. "We'll have to put our heads together and come up with another plan."

It was a quiet, albeit confident and composed, statement.

Patiently, Sousuke shook his head. "Listen, Chidori. I'm a specialist. There isn't any way for all three of us to escape this situation. It will be difficult for you to escape by yourself, even. That's the truth."

"Truth? Only according to you," she replied, slightly angry.

"But—"

"Enough!" Kaname's outburst dumbfounded Sousuke. "I've been doing a lot of thinking while we trudged through these mountains, and I've finally made up my mind."

Kaname paused to take a deep breath.

"Sagara, you really are a total idiot. I mean, I'm glad you want to save me, but aren't you forgetting something? I think you're missing something *extremely* important. Know what it is? I doubt it, because you're a complete dolt. I am not too keen on being saved by an idiot."

"Huh?" Sousuke hardly could believe his eyes and ears. Kaname was morphing from scared girl into domineering class president.

"Listen, you're always thinking stupid things like 'I don't care when I die.' You didn't even consider my feelings! You're just satisfying yourself, assaulting me with your good intentions. Do you think dying for my sake is cool or something? It's not cool, it's *idiotic!*

"If you sacrifice yourself for someone, it's only great if you understand your own importance before you do it. You've already devalued yourself. If you cared at all about yourself, you wouldn't give up so easily. You probably don't even feel like trying. Think about it. Forget duty for a minute and tell me: For whose sake are you saving me? And if you say mine, I will beat you to death!"

His head a jumbled mess, Sousuke stared at Kaname, who appeared to have fumed herself out. He was offended, astonished, embarrassed, amazed, and worried, all at once. He didn't totally understand what she meant, but he did grasp that she thought there was something wrong with him—and also that she was probably right.

As Sousuke struggled to find words, Kaname waved him off and said, "Forget it. I'll save us."

"Excuse me?"

"You said there was no other way, but I think that means that you've given up. That's why I have to do it. Do you have a lighter?"

"I do," he confirmed suspiciously. "What are you planning?"

"To set this mountain on fire," she announced. "A forest fire will cause an uproar. In the confusion, we'll steal a fire truck or a Jeep or something and high-tail it to the airport, where we'll steal a plane amid the confusion. Don't worry, I'll fly it."

"Do you have any experience flying an air—"

"Of course not! I've played the simulator at the arcade, though, so maybe I could figure it out. Anyway, once we have the plane, we'll go to South Korea or Japan. All we have to do is go south, right? Simple. You two just keep quiet and stay with me."

The holes in Kaname's logic were enormous, but she sounded deadly serious. An expression of courage in the face of tragedy rippled across her face.

"I'm never going to give up," she proclaimed, thumping her chest. "I'll never admit we can't save everyone. We'll do *something*. I'll get out of here with you and Kurz—and Kyouko and everyone else will be waiting when we get there. Then, we'll all live happily ever after. That's my plan. Got a problem with it?"

"Sometimes, willpower and enthusiasm won't cut it," Sousuke said. "Do as I say."

"How many times do I have to tell you 'no'?"

"Forget that. Go. Make a run for it." For good measure, he gestured at her with his submachine gun.

"Are you going to shoot me if I don't?" Kaname sounded almost sympathetic.

"Yes. You'd be better off dying here than getting caught by the enemy and turned into a vegetable."

"Well, that's a strange reason." Smiling, Kaname took a step toward Sousuke.

Why isn't she afraid? Sousuke was worried. He understood there was no way left to make her obey, and he was hopeless.

"Want to know why I'm not afraid?"

He grunted.

"It's simple," she cooed, pushing the gun aside to embrace Sousuke gently.

Sliding both hands around his back, she rested her cheek on his bloody shoulder.

"I trust you now."

For a moment, the warmth of the girl on Sousuke's chest overpowered the pain of his injury. Inside his body, all his blood seemingly switched directions and his muscles twitched. He didn't even notice when the gun slipped from his fingers.

"That's the reason I won't abandon you." Kaname's damp bangs tickled the tip of Sousuke's nose.

"Chidori . . ."

"I definitely was scared of you. It's terrifying to see a classmate turn into someone else. So strong . . ." she faltered, but she battled her hesitation. "But you asked me to trust you, right? I know you're just trying to save me, so I've told myself to trust you instead of fearing you. Isn't that great?"

"Yes, it is."

"If a simple high school student like me can overcome so much in order to trust you, you at least can try a little harder to value your own life. Let's go home together."

Go home together . . . with her. The thought was enormously appealing. If it were humanly possible, he wanted to try. How nice it would be to see her in the morning light, he imagined.

Why would he save her? For whose sake was he attempting it? He clearly understood it.

It's for me. I want to go home with her. I want to be with her. And live.

Realizing he never wanted anything as badly as this in his life, Sousuke felt an overwhelming power surge up through his exhausted and battered body.

"Chidori."

"Sagara."

They gazed awkwardly at each other.

"Um. Ahem," Kurz loudly and unapologetically cleared his throat, snapping Sousuke and Kaname back to Earth. They practically leapt away from each other.

"You . . . you're awake?" Kaname asked, disbelieving.

"A guy can't possibly get any sleep around here with you two shouting like that!"

"Why didn't you say something?"

Scratching his head, Kurz shrugged. "Don't know. Didn't seem like the thing to do. Seriously, though, you should keep it down. You guys, huh? How about that."

Blushing all the way to her ears, Kaname said, "Don't get the wrong idea. I just got carried away with the mood. Nothing was going to happen. Really!"

Was that what that was? Watching Kaname's over-the-top denial, Sousuke felt surprised.

Kurz could not keep himself from laughing any longer, which caused him to curse his injury. "You lose, Sousuke," he said. "'No' means 'no.' Your plan is vetoed, so you might want to consider hers."

"Meaning?"

"Start a forest fire or something. It isn't a bad idea—a lot better than dying here like this. Although, starting a fire could be difficult with all this rain, unless you have some gasoline with you. But even then, it'd still be a small fire."

"True—just big enough to give away our position."

"You don't know that. One of your planes could spot it just as easily," Kaname suggested.

"This is enemy airspace. Our people won't be flying here."

"Not even higher up? I saw it in a Harrison Ford movie once. There was this spy satellite watching from space. Don't you guys have any of those?"

Sousuke felt ill at ease about the prospect of disclosing classified information about Mithril's reconnaissance satellite, Sting, to an outsider. Given the circumstances, however, he broke protocol.

"We do. But we can't just tell it to fly over here. The satellite orbits are confidential, and noncommissioned officers like us aren't privy to them."

"Not exactly," mumbled Kurz. "Before moving out, I saw some satellite photos in the briefing. There were images of this base from yesterday at fifteen-hundred thirty hours. What time is it now?"

Checking his watch, Sousuke looked as if something struck him. "Two-hundred forty-eight hours. Nearly half a day later, which means . . ."

Generally, recon satellites revolved around the Earth once every ninety minutes. Factoring in the earth's rotation, the satellite passed over the same point about once every twelve hours. It if was over the base yesterday at fifteen-hundred thirty . . .

Sting's going to pass over here soon!

Knowing the approximate time of its arrival, perhaps they could announce their presence with flaming letters from the ground?

Exchanging glances, Kurz and Sousuke thought through the logistics of thermal landmarks in relation to recon satellites. And to think, the impetus of this idea came from the mouth of an amateur.

"What's wrong?" Kaname asked, her voice now tantamount to the loveliness of heaven in Sousuke's mind.

"Talk about a blind spot!"

"Kaname, you're the best!"

"I am? What are you talking about?"

However, the plan still was not a safe bet.

If they lit a fire, it could attract the satellite's attention—but it also could catch the enemy's eye. Meanwhile, even if their allies did see the sign, who knew whether a rescue team could reach the trio in time?

It probably would be safer for Kaname to flee solo. But she wanted to do this, to go home together.

It was worth a shot.

Riding, Sousuke slung the submachine gun back over his shoulder. "Let's do it, then. You stay here."

"Don't do anything—check!" said Kurz. "This is crazy, so it's perfect for you."

"Very true."

"Are you going alone Sagara? What about your shoulder?" asked Kaname.

"It's okay. I'll sneak around. Besides," he added, noting her concerned expression, "it's weird, but I have my energy back."

And with that, Sousuke abruptly disappeared into the darkness.

Once he was gone, Kaname wiped Kurz's dirty face with a spare scrap of cloth.

"Ha ha. Thanks, Kaname."

"You're welcome." She paused to reflect for a moment. "By the way, Kurz, do you know why they're after me?"

"All we know is that our boss ordered us to protect you."

"Okay." She hung her head and coughed a little.

Kaname felt quite heavy-headed. While she was talking to Sousuke, it wasn't significant enough to worry her. But now, an unpleasant sensation of floating crept over her.

When the odd visions she had experienced in the medical trailer intermittently attacked her, she couldn't determine whether they were a dream or reality.

"You okay?" wondered Kurz. "They give you any drugs back there?"

"Yeah. I don't know what it was, but they said something about a nutrient. Nothing really happened—but now, my head feels weird.

"Did they do anything else to you?"

"Yeah, they made me watch some kind of freaky movie."

"Movie?"

"Strange symbols and characters that kept replacing and overlapping one another. Even though I hadn't seen these words before, somehow I already knew them. They were things like 'raw materials of intervertebral disc dampers,' and 'reagents of palladium reactors,' and an explanation of how the invisibility mode of ECS is not totally perfected, because the burden is all on the laser screen oscillation system—"

"How do you know all this?" Kurz asked seriously, his eyes bulging.

"Huh?" asked Kaname as though coming out of a daze.

"Did you just say 'intervertebral disc dampers'?"

"Inter-what?"

"That's the name of a popular AS part—very technical stuff. No one without a military connection knows the weak points of ECS, either."

Kaname pressed her hands to her temples and tried to concentrate.

Slightly agitated, Kurz said, "There isn't any way a normal high school student would know these things."

"If you say so." Kaname wondered whether there was some kind of secret locked away inside her head. Then, she recalled the conversation with the female doctor in the trailer. "The lady kept saying strange things—that I knew that kind of stuff before I was born and that I had Black Technology or whatever. She said someday, I'd have free access to that information. Information . . ." Kaname drifted off, losing herself in an absentminded floating sensation. For the first time, she was voluntarily conscious of the *knowledge she was not yet aware of.*

"Information. Infor . . . ma-ma-ma . . . Ah." Nothing came to mind, but a vague sense of disgust settled into her chest.

Then, she had a sense of déjà vu, the hallucination a person might feel when traveling somewhere for the first time but finding it familiar. It was similar, except darker and heavier.

"Remem-memb-ber? Can't. C-can't," she stuttered, only slightly aware of herself and what she was saying.

There was a monster lurking in the shadows of Kaname's mind. The more she tried to examine it, the more some part of her (her soul itself, perhaps) convulsed. Up and down traded places, preventing her from thinking anymore. It was impossible. Impossible. Impossible . . .

"Impossible. Impossible. Wha—wh-what's this?" Kaname struggled terribly to suppress a hysterical scream.

"Kaname! Stop that! Look at me!" Kurz barked, bringing Kaname back to Earth.

She realized that she had torn the chest of her gown.

"What? What did I—? Wow, it looks like maybe I'm a little messed up. Ha ha ha. Ha ha." she attempted to make small talk while concealing her chest, but her voice sounded dead.

"Listen, Kaname. Don't think about that anymore. Forget the whole thing. Completely—ugh!" Kurz's face twisted in pain.

"You okay?"

After a moment, he said: "No, I'm not really." He tried to lift his head, but he couldn't really manage it. "Ah, this sucks. Son of a bitch, I can't believe I'm immobile at a time like this."

Moaning over his own helplessness, Kurz's blue eyes grew damp.

"It can't be helped." Kaname leaned in to wipe his tears. "You're hurt pretty bad."

"It really does suck. If I felt any better at all, I could admire it more carefully."

"Admire what?"

"Your cleavage."

When Sousuke came down the mountain, he could see the farmlands.

After creeping in, he extracted some engine oil from a decomposing tractor. He wanted gasoline, but the current economic crisis kept most tanks empty. The fact that this area still had a tractor at all indicated it was a prosperous region.

Holding the oil-filled, polyethylene tank, he ran to the farm's fallow land. His side throbbed, but it wasn't so bad that he couldn't endure it.

After dumping out the oil on the field, he checked his watch: Oh-three twenty-eight.

Here goes.

Taking the survival kit from his pocket, Sousuke procured a permanganic acid tablet that normally would be used for sterilizing. But he crushed it, spread the powder on the oil, and lit the mixture with a Zippo.

After a second, the oil ignited, and the flames slowly spread.

Sting, the recon satellite, took extremely high-resolution pictures. On a clear day, it could easily read the headline on a newspaper. On a drizzly night like this, however, it would be difficult to distinguish Sousuke and friends from local soldiers. That's why Sousuke used fire letters to spell out A67ALIVE.

The A was for "Angel," Kaname's codename. The numbers were for "Urzu Six" and "Urzu 7," Kurz and Sousuke, respectively. "Alive" was self-explanatory, really.

Mindful not to leave footprints, Sousuke returned to Kurz and Kaname.

There was no need to indicate their location. If Sting saw those letters, it could follow Sousuke's fire-lit silhouette from space.

The oil fire probably would die in just a few minutes, and there was no guarantee that either allies or enemies would see it. It was, after all, a gamble.

April 29, 03:45 (Japan/Korea Standard Time)
Democratic People's Republic of Korea
Sunan Air Base

"Arson?" asked Gauron.

Standing in front of a maintenance trailer where he was overseeing the Codarl's repairs, Gauron looked over the report from his subordinate.

"Yes, sir. We just got word that someone set fire to a field on a farm nine miles west of here."

Gauron harrumphed. He wondered if it was a diversion, but he decided that it was unlikely, as a simple fire wouldn't suffice. Regardless, he figured Kashim was the likely culprit. Even if Gauron didn't know what Kashim was up to, at least he knew the vicinity of his whereabouts.

"The military already is tightening their search radius. It's only a matter of time before we discover the escapees."

"Kill the man. As for the girl, they can do with her as they like, as long as she is not killed under any circumstances."

"Yes, sir."

"I'll be moving out soon, as well."

"In the Codarl?"

Gauron glared. "You got a problem with that?"

"C-certainly not, sir. But Doctor Kaneyama said you shouldn't use it much in front of the local soldiers."

"It isn't forbidden. Besides, we're up against Mithril—and Kalinin. There could be trouble still."

According to the naval report, Mithril's submarine already had fled away from the coast to nearby Chinese waters. Even if they used their urgent deployment boosters, dispatching a rescue party seemed impossible. But still . . .

"Better safe than sorry. Get me?"

Right on cue, an engineer closed the maintenance hatch and shouted that the repairs were complete.

April 29, 03:55 (Japan/Korea Standard Time)
Democratic People's Republic of Korea
Mountains of Taedong County, South Pyongan Province

When Sousuke returned, Kaname seemed relieved to see him. She tightly clutched her shirt across her chest, where it had been torn open somehow. Kurz appeared to be sleeping.

"How is he?"

"Unexpectedly well, I'd say. *His* type lives a long time."

Unsure what that meant and how to respond, Sousuke took a seat on a tree root.

"Well? Will it work?"

"I don't know. It's a long shot, at best. I still think it would be easier for you to escape alone."

"Too late now. I don't feel like reconsidering, anyway."

"I know. I won't say it again."

"Thanks."

In the distance, helicopter rotors hacked at the sky. They didn't seem to be approaching—and ten seconds later, the sound faded.

Like a desolate maze with no exit, the dark woods were gloomy.

Kaname broke the silence. "Hey, if . . . if we get back okay, what are you going to do, Sagara?"

"Take on the next mission."

"You mean you'll go off somewhere else? You won't go to school anymore?"

"Probably not. It was just a temporary assignment for me to be a student. It definitely would get in the way of other duties. I'll probably just disappear."

"Oh . . ."

Sousuke's ears perked up as he heard footsteps.

They were much quicker and quieter than a human's. Wild breathing suggested it was some kind of animal—maybe a dog.

Then, from a distance, he also heard human footsteps: three, four people, maybe more.

Sousuke held his breath; meanwhile, the sound of twigs snapping underfoot grew closer. There was a frenzied howl.

"What's—"

"They're coming. Stay down," commanded Sousuke.

Almost immediately, two dogs leapt out from behind a rock. It was too dark to tell what kind of dogs they were, but they were big and black and headed straight at them.

Without hesitation, Sousuke fired. The dogs yelped. One of the dogs had enough momentum that it slammed into a squealing Kaname. However, a moment later, it writhed and died.

Hearing the shots, the pursuit squad opened fire from somewhere in the forest. White lines traced bullet paths, rocks shattered, and dead branches rained from the trees.

"They followed you, you dumbass!" reprimanded Kurz.

"Only a matter of time—can't help it," shrugged Sousuke. With their injuries and available equipment, there was no masking the scent of blood.

A soldier appeared, taking in the situation from the shadow of a huge tree. Sousuke aimed at his legs and fired once. His aim was true. Purposefully, he fired a couple of shots in the area where the soldier fell. The soldier screamed, seeking help from his comrades, and another soldier who was willing to die for his friend rushed toward the wounded one, dragging him toward a pine bower.

"There's at least two."

"Just *kill* 'em," grumbled Kurz. "Damn."

The enemy fire picked up. Reinforcements.

"At this rate, there'll be mechs here soon."

"So this is it." Kurz burst into laughter.

Sousuke had no more than ten rounds left in his gun.

"Looks like it was hopeless after all, eh?" mumbled Kaname.

"It appears that way. Sorry," Sousuke said, returning fire.

"I don't regret it," Kaname announced, trying to sound cheerful.

"Okay."

"I'm glad I met you, Sagara."

After a moment, Sousuke responded in a dark voice. "Yeah."

He ran out of ammo. Now, Sousuke's combat would be limited to bludgeoning people with the bulletless gun.

Kurz groaned. "The end!"

"No," corrected Sousuke, keeping an eye on the sky. "Aerial reinforcements."

Three-hundred feet over their heads, a parachuting capsule burst open.

Sparks from the explosive bolts scattered, illuminated a white AS dancing in the black sky.

The mech raised both arms over its head in midair, as if trying to balance itself, and reached terminal velocity.

"Here it comes."

In front of their eyes, the AS landed just fifteen feet ahead of them on the slope. Mud and pebbles shot in all directions, and its massive drive system emitted a grinding sound. White steam—evaporating shock absorbent—discharged from several of the machine's joints, creating a temporary fog.

The three of them gaped at the AS, which was white as snow.

"What is this?"

Although its frame resembled that of an M9, the shape of the armor was different. By nature, Arm Slaves took an aircraftlike form—but with this mech, the trend was even more pronounced: Its sharp silhouette suggested the frenzy of a raptor. It was sharp like a knife, and there was a sense of tension in the air.

This machine had the kind of cold ferocity that suggested that, once it found its prey, there would be no escape.

"Land war weapon" was not an adequate description; it was the world's most dangerous work of art.

On its hip pylon—the equipment fixture—was a shot cannon. In the armpit pylon were spare magazines and a monofilament blade.

"Who's in that thing? Mao?"

For that matter, where was everyone? Did they really send just one mech?

As if to answer these questions, the AS knelt and its cockpit hatch opened.

Oddly, no one emerged.

The white AS remained in its pose. After several seconds, nothing changed. Enemy gunfire hit the armor plate on occasion—but even then, the mech didn't move an inch.

"Hey, you don't suppose—"

Before Kurz could finish his sentence, Sousuke darted toward the white AS. Nimbly climbing up to the cockpit, he narrowly avoided bullets, which he didn't have time to worry about. He checked inside.

"Unmanned."

The empty cockpit was mostly the same as that of an M9 or any other AS, so there was room enough for only one person to fit snugly. Sousuke went ahead and slid inside. The forward multipurpose screen lit up, indicating the machine was ready to go at anytime.

"Commencing voice-print check. State your name, rank, and identification number," requested the mech's AI. It had a deep, male voice.

"Sergeant Sousuke Sagara. B3128."

"Comparison complete. Identity confirmed. Your orders?"

"Close the hatch. Begin tuning to mode four. Bilateral angle: three point five."

"Roger. Run mode four. BMSA three point five: completed," recited the machine.

The hatch closed immediately, and the semi-master/slave control system started up. Now, Sousuke's arms practically were the same as the machine's.

I can do this. This white AS is pretty much the same as the M9.

Sousuke stood the AS up.

"Start with the chain gun."

"Roger," affirmed the AS.

The machine guns mounted on the head roared as hundreds of rounds per second spewed forth, instantly tearing the surrounding pine trees to confetti, inspiring enemy soldiers to flee.

It was nearly an instant reversal of the situation. Dumbstruck, Kaname and Kurz looked up at the mech.

That's when the red letters in the corner of the screen caught Sousuke's eye.

Inspect data recorder's prep file. A1—highest priority.

263

Sousuke instructed the computer to play back the data, and Kalinin's voice filled the cockpit.

"Sergeant Sagara. If you can hear this recording, it means you successfully rendezvoused with this AS. Now, I'll tell you the reason for this: When Sting discovered your group, the de Danaan was forty miles from shore. This was too far to dispatch a regular rescue squad, so we used a modified ballistic missile to send this AS. That's why it was unmanned."

"Okay." said Sousuke.

A ballistic missile could cover that distance in just a few minutes, but it couldn't carry a person because the G-force at launch would not be kind to a human body.

"Under radio silence, the de Danaan is headed toward the West Korea Bay Coast," continued Kalinin's message. "We plan to skim the coast, recover your group, and escape at full speed. Find a way to make it to the indicated point by that time."

A digital map showed the recovery point, just south of a village called Hasanbuk, which was about twelve miles from their current location.

The current time was oh-four hundred thirteen, leaving seventeen minutes until their allies could make it to shore.

"Furthermore, this AS is called the ARX-7 Arbalest. The AI's call sign is Al. It's a highly valuable test unit, so be sure to bring it back. That is all. Good luck," concluded Kalinin.

The ARX-7 Arbalest, huh?

Sousuke checked the machine's condition. Energy surged from its palladium reactor, power swelling its electromagnetic muscles. He could feel its superiority, even in tiny movements.

"Enemy mechs approaching. Five estimated," warned Al. The screen projected the assumed positions and distances of the enemy units, which were ahead to the left and right. They were approaching at high speed, presumably to surround the Arbalest.

The auditory sensor detected the deep menacing roar of the enemy units' gas turbine engines.

The optical sensor cut through the darkness, picking up signs of the enemy—khaki armor with two red eyes.

Rk-92 Savages.

Sliding along the mountain ridge, the Savages kept their rifles ready. They didn't look like they were going to give up and run. After all, they outnumbered Sousuke five to one.

But it was up to him what would happen next. He *would* take Kaname home. He found the pain of his wound oddly comforting.

"Al, right?"

"Yes, Sergeant."

"We're going to do this in one minute or less."

"Roger."

Just like that, the Arbalest leapt.

"Ew!"

The mud Sousuke's AS kicked up pelted Kaname and Kurz.

When it was safe to open their eyes again, the white AS had already landed behind the mountain, where it charged at the approaching enemy.

Had it really gone that far in an instant? Even to Kaname's untrained eyes, it was clear that the mech was a cutting-edge machine with extraordinary jumping power. The khaki Arm Slaves wouldn't stand a chance.

"Wow."

From their position, Kaname and Kurz could make out two enemy units, which were hopping around on the dark slope to engage Sousuke's AS.

One of the enemy mechs fired its rifle, and Kaname gasped.

The next instant, however, the enemy blew apart, and neither Kaname nor Kurz could tell how it had happened.

Approaching the other mech like a hopping bird, the white AS belched a white light as it passed. Sousuke must have fired. The blast spun the enemy in midair, sending it crashing to the ground, where it exploded.

After that, the hill obscured Kaname's view.

Running through a ravine, the white AS danced through the air. Just when it appeared about to collide with an enemy, it sprang over it. Countless fireballs scorched the night sky, seeking the leaping mech.

In the darkness, it resembled a spark leaping about at will.

"It's like a ninja manga," commented Kaname.

Kaname and Kurz couldn't see how many enemy units there were, but it sure sounded as if there were more than four. Sousuke shot them all, leaving them in pieces.

Lightning fast, Sousuke rushed the last enemy mech, firing two rounds from the shot cannon.

"And that's five!" he panted as the enemy vehicle fell to the ground, bleeding smoke.

It took exactly fifty-eight seconds for Sousuke to silence the pursuing enemy AS squad. With catlike alertness, he scanned for signs of an ambush. After ten seconds, he was convinced there were no more enemy mechs.

Good, now's our chance.

Intending to collect the others and escape, Sousuke returned to Kurz and Kaname.

But then, a silver AS popped out of a mountain recess to the right.

From point-blank range, it rapidly fired its carbine rifle with raging hostility.

Rolling his mech forward, Sousuke barely evaded the line of fire before he counterattacked with the shot cannon. The enemy seemed to anticipate this and dodged. It jumped and fired three pinpoint-accurate shots. The Arbalest kept rolling forward, somehow managing to survive.

With a grating laugh, the silver AS landed. He was using the external speaker.

"Nicely done, Kashim!"

Gauron fired his rifle again, and Sousuke shot back. They both missed, tearing trees from their roots.

Most AS battles lasted just two or three shots. One had to make the best choice, whether it was to stop and snipe, keep moving and fire containment rounds, or focus on evasive maneuvers. These decisions had to be made quickly, on the fly. And the first to make a mistake instantly would suffer fatal damage.

The fight between these two was different.

Neither yielded an inch. Never resting, they ran, jumped, ducked, rolled, and fired—again and again. Each and every shell missed. No matter how intensely they moved, the machine limbs didn't tire. This battle would end only with the destruction of one of the mechs—or one of the pilot's nerves.

It was a furious dogfight, but it was on the ground.

"That silver AS is the same one from earlier," Kaname noted absentmindedly.

The white and silver puppets popped in and out of her view. Just when she thought they were behind the mountain, a burst of flames signaled their position behind a rock on the other side. They leapt, mowed down trees, and colored dark ravines red.

"Keep low," advised Kurz. "A fragment or stray bullet would be fatal."

Kaname ignored Kurz, standing completely still as if watching far-off fireworks.

"Which one's superior?"

"In normal combat, they should be equal. However . . ."

"However?"

"That silver AS isn't normal. It has a secret."

"That's the one that beat you?" she asked, taking her eyes off the battle.

"Yeah. My shell flew off in midair, you know. I don't know what kind of trick—"

"It's not a trick," Kaname declared. Her head felt heavy, and the eerie sense of floating enveloped her again. She heard the whispering voice.

Reverberating through her skull, the voice told her that what Kurz said wasn't right. It wasn't a trick contained in that AS. It was something else.

"Not . . . a trick. It's technology."

The enemy had it—in *his* mech.

"He'll lose," she stated.

"What?"

"At this rate Sousuke's going to lose."

A grenade Gauron lobbed exploded in uncomfortably close proximity.

The Arbalest ducked to avoid the blast and any shrapnel. Then, appearing to stand up, it grabbed a fallen tree and flung it.

When the tree crashed to the ground in between the two mechs, they could no longer see each other. At that instant, although neither could see the other, they fired simultaneously.

Conifers blew apart.

The Arbalest took a hit on the lower-right part of its head. Machine-gun ammo went off, and half of the main sensors were destroyed. Gauron's AS, on the other hand, sustained damage to its rifle; the binary liquid tank ruptured, and it broke down completely.

In terms of damage to the mechs, the Arbalest was in more serious condition. However . . .

I win.

Sousuke still had weapons. It was close range, and he would not miss.

Sousuke blasted away with his shot cannon. Gauron's mech still staggered from the previous attack. The small warhead flew from the barrel, separated into eight pieces, and continued toward the other mech's torso.

Sousuke didn't believe what he saw next: Every piece of the shot shattered before hitting Gauron's AS, as if it were crashing into an invisible wall. Sousuke didn't understand.

Shortly after that, a violent shock rocked the Arbalest. It seemed as though a great force were pulling Sousuke forward, but then it threw him back.

The Arbalest arced through the air, spun, and tumbled shoulder first to the surface.

Gauron's loud laughter resounded through the ravine.

"Dammit, there it was," lamented Kurz.

From a faraway vantage point, it still looked like some incomprehensible phenomenon.

It couldn't have been a fragmentation mine, nor explosive reactive armor. It was a force field and some kind of shockwave. There simply was no other way to describe it.

The white AS didn't move.

Although Kurz and Kaname couldn't see it, they imagined it to be damaged. After all, an M9 in good condition had been blown to pieces from the same device, so this prototype surely couldn't withstand it.

Kaname remained still.

"Oh, God," she pleaded.

Sousuke gasped, shaking his head. He literally was seeing red; it must have been "red out" from the G-force of the crash. His whole body felt numb, and he barely could move his fingertips. His side felt wet, indicating that his wound had reopened.

He remembered Kurz's words: "It was like being hit with a hammer."

So, *this* is what he had meant.

He knew Kurz's mech had been destroyed by a hit like that, so Sousuke assumed that his was in a similar state. There was no way it could be functional after that kind of shock. His AS had lost. He had lost to Gauron.

This time, it really is the end.

After a moment, his reddened vision returned to normal, and he studied the on-screen letters. Blue letters.

Contrary to his expectations, the screen read: "Damage slight—no hindrance to combat."

Now, it was Gauron's turn to question *his* eyes: With great effort, the white AS sat up. And then it stood.

Although the head was partially destroyed, the machine appeared to be otherwise unharmed. The Mithril AS that Gauron had defeated earlier had blown apart completely!

"Ah! Why didn't that work?"

Shaking his head, Gauron checked his drive system. He used the Lambda Driver properly—having charged its personal condenser—so it wasn't an output problem.

"A misfire? Weird."

In any case, it was an imperfect device; at times, it did not operate as desired.

The personal condensers were in a cylinder like a six-shooter, and Gauron revolved it, causing a new one to lock into place.

"There." Gauron chuckled, planning to attack with the Lambda Driver again. This time, he'd make sure to get the job done.

"What's going on?" wondered Sousuke, still in awe of the damage report.

Outside of the head damage, the machine virtually was unharmed.

"How the hell . . .?"

It sounded like something was turning around on the Arbalest's back—some kind of cylinder. Then, there was the sharp sound of something connecting.

"What did you do? What's that movement?"

Ignoring those questions, Al said, "Lambda Driver initialized."

"What? What are you talking about?"

"Unable to respond. Resuming combat."

"Answer me, Al."

"Unable to respond."

On the screen, Gauron's AS unsheathed its knifelike monofilament blade.

"He's alive? How the hell?" Kurz was gobsmacked.

Kurz wondered why Sousuke was okay when his own mech had been obliterated.

"Oh, okay," Kaname began, putting her hand to her temple. "S-somehow . . . I get it."

"Kaname? Are you okay? Hey."

Supporting herself on a tree trunk, Kaname coughed a few times before gazing at the white AS in the distance.

"I feel sick. The TAROS . . . he doesn't . . . understand how to use it." Her dainty shoulders heaved up and down as she mumbled frail incoherencies. "Only keeping up . . . with his opponent. Strong self-defense urge . . ."

Kaname's eyes looked far from sane, the same way they had appeared earlier.

"Get a grip, Kaname. Cut it out!"

"Can't. I've got to . . . i-instruct . . ."

"Instruct? What are you talk—"

"Always being saved . . . not this time . . . must instruct."

Finally, Kurz understood Kaname's cryptic ramblings. She knew something valuable that could help overcome the enemy. It seemed as if she were wrestling her own mind to extract the information.

"Pseudo . . . lam . . . fa, fa, fa." She sobbed in apparent anguish. "Ph-phase interference is th-the t-t-TAROS . . . Hn . . . ah. No. N-n. But not."

Kaname grabbed her disheveled hair and arched her back.

Kurz couldn't help getting the willies from the manifestation of her madness.

"Hey!" he called, but she did not respond.

"I . . . won't lose!"

With that, Kaname bashed her head against the tree trunk. The recoil knocked her down, and she rocked back and forth vigorously. Curving her body backward, she spewed gibberish in an inverted crying voice.

"Kaname!" Kurz thought he might go crazy, too, just from watching. *What the hell is this? I'm a soldier, not a nurse in a nut house! What am I supposed to do about something like this?*

"Ha! Ha. K-Kurz . . ." Kaname stood in front of Kurz and attempted to speak, but she couldn't quite inspire her tongue to the task. She glared at him with ghastly eyes, inhaled, and said, "Ku-Kurz. G-give me your transmitter."

It was entirely urgent, a different tone from before.

"Fine by me, but why——"

"I must hurry and tell him."

"Tell him what?"

"Hurry!"

No matter how many times Sousuke asked, the Arbalest's AI would not answer his question.

It was no time to bicker: The enemy approached. Having already dropped his shot cannon during the last impact, Sousuke extracted the monofilament blade from the mech's armpit.

But if he does that to me again . . .

Even if the mech survived, Sousuke's body couldn't take another shot like that. With that thought, his whole body broke out in a sweat.

Suddenly, he heard a new voice—a short-range transmission from outside.

"Sagara, can you hear me?"

"Chidori?"

"Listen carefully! Your enemy has special equipment."

Kaname's voice was hoarse, as if being wrung out of her, and Sousuke wondered if she was wounded.

"It's a mechanism that converts the pilot's attack impulses into physical power. This is im-imporant."

"Chido—"

"L-listen. And . . . I don't know why, but your AS also is equipped with a Lambda Driver. That's why you're still alive!"

Lambda Driver? That's the phrase the Arbalest used.

Gauron's AS was only about a hundred feet away now.

"Surely, you thought about protecting yourself, right? The mechanism reacted to that. With it, strong images in your mind take shape!"

"Images? In my mind? No weapon like that could ever—"

Stopping in front of the Arbalest, Gauron's AS glared with one red eye. With no warning, the surrounding atmosphere waved and distorted.

Trees, grass, mud, and rocks flew about as though hit by an intense gust. It was another shockwave. There was no stopping it—in the blink of an eye, it hit the Arbalest.

"Oh!"

The top half of the mech bent back. However, this time, it was not as bad as Sousuke expected. After taking several steps back to steady itself, the Arbalest regained its posture.

"Was that it?"

"Yes. Your opponent thought he would break you into pieces just now, but he wasn't able to. You can counterattack, too. Focus hard!"

"Focus on what?"

"Think about taking out your opponent. Put your spirit into it, all at once, like a *kamehameha* or something!"

"Kameha-what?"

"Proximity warning!" alerted Al.

Bearing in, the silver AS thrust its knife. The Arbalest barely managed to stave it off.

Inside his mech, Gauron laughed. "That just might be it!"

He took a few swipes at Sousuke, and they began a dizzying knife fight.

"You're protecting a Whispered! No wonder you have *it*."

"What?"

"You know my specialty is knives, right?"

Thrust, parry, slash, strike, lure, resist!

Every time a monofilament blade grazed armor, white light illuminated the area.

"Come on, don't be so slow!"

Gauron's attacks were fierce and skillful enough that an ordinary pilot and AS wouldn't have lasted three seconds. With his mech's main sensor half-destroyed, Sousuke gradually lost ground.

"Do you remember how I hacked those villagers to pieces, Kashim? Like this!"

Gauron's knife cut through the Arbalest's chest armor.

"Come on, put some spirit into it!" Kaname shouted through the wireless.

"I've *been* doing that! I can't just make a force field!"

"Here's how you use it!" Gauron shouted, right before a large shock hit Sousuke.

Falling backward, the Arbalest rolled a few times. Sousuke's vision went dark, and stars flickered in his head. Still, though, he was able to get right back up. This time, he adopted a defensive stance against the incoming mech.

Laughing sadistically, Gauron seemed to enjoy making sport of Sousuke.

"Ha ha! It's absurd: Two grown men killing each other with toys they don't really even know how to use, eh?"

Seeing the shot cannon he dropped earlier about a hundred feet away, Sousuke made his mech crawl toward it to pick it up again.

"Oh, ho! What are you going to do with that? Shoot me?"

Sousuke grunted.

"You know it's pointless, right? I mean, you barely even know how to use your equipment!"

This was undeniably true. Even if Sousuke fired the shot cannon here, Gauron easily could use another force field to reflect the shells. To some degree, at least, Gauron understood the principles of the system, and he appeared to be experienced at handling it. This was not the case for Sousuke.

Withstanding Gauron's attacks was about all he could do.

Skillfully, the silver AS twirled its knife as it approached the Arbalest at a leisurely pace.

The next time it came in, Sousuke probably wouldn't be able to fully defend himself. The cockpit would be pierced, and Sousuke would be done for.

"Listen, Sagara," urged Kaname. "The important part is momentary concentration! Breathe in slowly, and then breathe out all at once. In that instant, envision your own willpower going into the shell!"

"That's easy for you to say."

He couldn't do it. Sousuke couldn't apply Kaname's advice.

"Then think about this: If you lose, I'll be captured and stripped naked; then, they'll do who knows what to me before they kill me. Just put that vision in your head!"

"What?"

"Just do it!"

He wasn't sure what to say—just thinking about it was terrible.

"You don't like it, do you?"

"No."

"Does it make you angry?"

"Of course."

"Well, *he* is trying to do *that* to me! Are you going to let him?"

Slowly, the sense of crisis driving Sousuke fell victim to his anger. "I won't!"

"That's right. Point your gun at him!"

Following orders, Sousuke aimed the shot cannon at the enemy mech. Temporarily, he forgot that it was a useless act. It didn't matter what would come of this, nor what Kaname knew.

She trusted me. Now, it's time for me to trust her.

"Desperate, huh? I'm disappointed, Kashim. I guess it's time for you to die!"

Intending to finish the fight, Gauron rushed at the Arbalest with his knife out.

"It's okay," Kaname cooed. "Just close your eyes and concentrate on this image: You're about to hit him barehanded."

Although it was the height of recklessness to close your eyes in the face of the enemy, Sousuke did as he was told. When the AI warned of the enemy mech's approach, it fell on deaf ears.

The sight of him punching the silver AS came to mind.

"Now open your eyes."

Right in front of Sousuke's shot cannon, the enemy mech charged, filling Sousuke's entire display screen.

"Rot in hell!" Gauron shouted ferociously.

"Breathe in," Kaname instructed gently.

Sousuke took a deep breath.

"Envision it."

He pictured his whole will going into the shell.

"Now!"

Sousuke grunted. There was a point-blank shot.

In defense, Gauron's mech emitted another shockwave. But, at the same time, Sousuke's image took shape, and the Arbalest's unknown powers kicked in.

Sousuke couldn't tell exactly what happened.

What he could tell was that two things collided. The air twisted, distorted, and screeched. Temporarily, gravity seemed arbitrary.

Ultimately, the bullet did not stop—it hit the silver AS.

"What?"

As the 00-HESH round struck Gauron's mech, it split into eight pieces. While the AS stumbled backward, one of its arms fell off and exploded.

The blast sent the Arbalest rolling, as well. Scattered debris pelted the armor plate with a dry clang.

Under the rain, flame, and wind, Sousuke sat up in his mech.

Gauron's AS was damaged severely. The head and both arms were obliterated, and the majority of the chest was destroyed. The giant, so full of frenzied life just moments ago, was scrap metal now.

Certainly, Gauron must have died instantly.

"Sagara, are you okay?"

"Affirmative."

Turning his back on the wreckage, Sousuke ran the mech toward Kaname and Kurz.

"I'm heading back your way. We need to go."

They had to hurry—the battle had taken nearly five minutes.

As soon as he reached the others, Sousuke made the AS kneel.

"How are you feeling, Chidori?"

"Better than before. I've practically forgotten what I was talking about, though."

It was good of her to give him advice; Sousuke shuddered to think what might have happened to him if not for her help.

Helicopters roared from the east, announcing the coming of pursuit reinforcements.

"Let's move. We don't have time."

With that, Sousuke fixed the shot cannon to the Arbalest's hip, picked up Kurz and Kaname in its open hands, and took off running. Twelve miles in ten minutes . . . with this mech, they could make it.

Clutching the passengers, the Arbalest crossed the mountain slope in one bound. Kicking up pebbles and uprooting shrubs, it rushed out onto level farmland.

"Gah!" Kurz agonized. He was in extremely intense pain.

Sousuke operated the mech carefully, keeping the speed down to about seventy-five miles per hour. Even so, there was no way to eliminate the pitching completely. An AS probably was the least adroit vehicle for transporting the wounded.

Trampling paddy fields, the Arbalest kept running west, encountering several armored vehicles, which Sousuke ignored. Whizzing bullets did not faze him; he just kept running.

When they were still a couple of miles from the coast, the AI spoke. "One attack helicopter, range eight, at your seven."

The heat signature on the rear-warning sensor indicated a chopper was coming for them.

"Here they come!"

"Rocket alert! Two, one . . ."

In an emergency maneuver, Sousuke swung the mech wide to the right, avoiding the incoming air-to-ground rocket.

Kurz let out a little scream, which overlapped the sound of the rocket exploding.

"Enemy helicopter closing at relative velocity of eighty. Must return fire," said Al.

"I know that!"

When the helicopter unleashed another rocket, Sousuke barely evaded it. If it got any closer, he would be unable to dodge.

What do I do?

With Sousuke traveling only seventy-five miles per hour, the chopper caught up in the blink of an eye. But Sousuke couldn't use the shot cannon: His hands were otherwise occupied, with Kaname in the right and Kurz in the left. There was no time to set them down—the helicopter would be there too quickly.

"Kaname!"

"Uh, what?"

"Sorry!"

While still sprinting, the Arbalest heaved Kaname's body high into the air. With its free right hand, it drew the gun, turned, and fired two shots.

After tossing the gun aside, Sousuke made the mech dash forward madly.

"Aieeee!" It was the parabolic scream of someone falling through the air.

At the last second, just before Kaname splatted into the ground, Sousuke scooped up her body, putting all his concentration into controlling the mech as it started to tumble.

Concurrently, the shattered attack helicopter crashed into a field and exploded. Sousuke kept running.

"Kaname?" he called.

No response.

A little grunt indicated she was breathing, though likely unconscious. He would have to wait to administer first aid and an apology. For now, they had only one minute to get to shore.

"There it is!"

Under the deep night sky, the sea looked darker than black. There was a sandy beach to the right and a cape to the left; Sousuke drove the mech toward the cape.

"Two mechs, range six, at your eleven," chirped Al.

There they were: two Savages up on the cape, probably out on coastal watch. There also was an enemy unit from the direction of the beach. Surrounding Sousuke, there were all together at least four or five mechs—no, more.

An AS was quite a different enemy than an attack helicopter. And besides, Sousuke had almost no means of attacking. He considered the strange force-field emitter unreliable.

"Crap!"

Loading its rifle, the enemy's lead mech turned to face Sousuke.

"Urzu Seven, run straight ahead," instructed a woman on the radio.

"Ma—"

Before Sousuke even finished saying Mao's name, the two mechs in front of him burst into flames and collapsed.

It was a sniper from the ocean! Closer inspection revealed an AS with a large rifle about a thousand feet from the shore. Mao's M9 appeared to be kneeling on the sea.

Then, beneath it, the Tuatha de Danaan surfaced, cleaving the inky water.

"Sousuke? You have just one chance: Jump directly from the tip of the cape!" instructed Mao.

Leaving two enemy AS divisions in the dust, the Arbalest ran into a rocky area of the beach. It climbed a rocky slope. Really, the cape resembled a giant ski jump.

As debris flew all around, the pursuers fired, destroying pine trees left and right. Sousuke accelerated without looking back.

Suddenly, the end of the cape loomed. Ahead of it, there was a cliff—beyond that, the sea. Carefully cradling his passengers, Sousuke concentrated.

As he leapt, the ground disappeared beneath his legs, and his body felt weightless. There were only dark waves beneath him now.

The de Danaan approached quickly. Mao's M9 waited with outstretched arms.

"All right!" hooted Mao, catching the incoming Arbalest. "Urzu Seven recovered! Admission from hatch four: complete!"

"Hatch four closure commencing! Two more seconds," reported the duty officer, whose screen read *secrecy maintenance.* "Closure complete."

Teletha Testarossa nodded and said: "Hard to starboard, course 205, full combat speed. Mind the depth, please!"

"Aye aye, ma'am. Hard to starboard, course 205," echoed the navigation officer. "Maximum speed!"

The ship lurched right, chopping through the surface waves. Enemy fire splashed haphazardly around it.

The screen's velocity display shot up past fifty knots, close to thirty-five miles per hour.

The fastest any normal submarine could travel was forty knots, but the de Danaan easily broke through that barrier. The on-screen speedometer continued to increase.

"Present speed, sixty-five knots."

Seventy-five miles per hour!

This freakish cruising ability was what enabled the de Danaan to get to the coast in such a short amount of time.

Quickly, the ship fled the coast.

"When we reach a depth of one-hundred sixty-five feet, flood the main ballast tank and set the diving angle to five degrees," ordered the navigation officer. "Maintain present speed."

"Aye! Beginning planned dive," responded the helm officer.

Tessa and Mardukas closely watched the diving procedures.

"This is the first time we've pushed it this hard," Mardukas commented.

"The super-conducting propulsion system?" clarified Tessa.

The executive officer nodded and said, "Yes, ma'am. It seems tough. From our preliminary tests, I thought it would be more delicate."

"I'm surprised, too." Tessa smiled and looked at her screen before adding, "I guess that's strange for its creator to say, isn't it?"

She returned her attention to passing a series of patrol boats.

Freshly patched up, Sousuke returned to the hangar.

Kaname and Kurz both were conked out in the medical office still.

The hangar was quiet; noise regulations throughout the ship prohibited the maintenance crew from working there.

Covered in bandages, Sousuke gazed at the kneeling ARX-7 Arbalest. Splotches of mud and grass stains marred the white exterior. The armor was a mess, and the lower right part of the head was missing.

In this light, it was just an AS—an eccentric prototype mech based on the M9 Gernsback. But what on Earth was . . .

"Looking pretty terrible," declared the lieutenant commander, approaching from behind Sousuke. "What happened to Gauron?"

"He died. No mistake this time."

"I see. I wish I could have been there for that." Kalinin sighed. "You look like you have more to say."

"Yes, sir. What exactly is the Lambda Driver?"

Kalinin seemed prepared to answer this frank question. "I heard rumors Gauron had one."

"Yes, he did. And this AS has one, too, if I'm not mistaken."

"You're correct. When I heard that Weber's M9 got totaled, I knew it was a possibility. That's why I sent the Arbalest. It takes an AS with that kind of firepower to stop one of the same."

Now Sousuke understood why they had flung an unmanned, highly valuable, experimental mech into enemy territory.

"That still doesn't answer my question," persisted Sousuke, "about the Lambda Driver."

"You don't need to know. Not at this stage."

"Lieutenant Commander, I am aware of rudimentary physics, but I've never heard of a device with powers like that."

"Of course not. No one in this world has thought of it."

"What do you mean?"

"Your generation probably hasn't realized it," Kalinin said heavily, "but today's weapon technology is abnormal. It started with the AS. The Lambda Driver, ECS, this ship's propulsion system, sensors—it's all *overdeveloped.* Any way you look at it, it's weird. Don't you ever think it's strange that sci-fi robots dominate the battlefields?"

Commanding a mechanized assault division was an everyday activity for Kalinin, so Sousuke was surprised to hear him say something like that.

"Today, I thought so for the first time," answered Sousuke.

"I've felt it for a long time—many people think weapons like this shouldn't exist. But the reality is that they do. I don't know who thought them up, but the theories and technologies are real. And society understands that."

Sousuke didn't know what to say.

"But, as I said, *things like this really shouldn't exist.*" Kalinin stared at the Arbalest, finding the indispensable mechanical ally somewhat grotesque. "Who the hell dreamed up this technology—Black Technology—that drives current weapons, like the AS? Do you know where it came from?"

"Perhaps people like Chidori? The ones called the Whispered."

"I'm not allowed to say, but it's possible." Kalinin walked over to get a closer look at the Arbalest's damage. "In regards to Chidori, the intelligence bureau will handle the situation by spreading false information."

"False information?"

"Most likely that Gauron's group investigated her and she turned out to be a non-Whispered. She should be safe, but we'll still have to be ready in case an enemy wants to kidnap her. We'll destroy their bases and rescue her as many times as we have to."

Kaname might be able to live a normal life.

The idea appealed to Sousuke, but he still felt a great sense of loss. His next mission awaited, and there would no longer be a place for him in Kaname's life. He felt Jindai High School, its hallways, and its people quickly fading.

"However," Kalinin began, interrupting Sousuke's thoughts, "this incident was a good precedent. It'll be easier to have *insurance*."

"Sir?"

"You've done well. Get some rest."

With that, Lieutenant Commander Kalinin walked away.

Epilogue

Hurtling toward the earth, Kaname saw a large, steel hand come out of nowhere.

Huh? The next time Kaname opened her eyes, they were pressed into a white pillow. The IV stand next to her did not block her view of a rectangular window, which presented a pleasant view of a damp cherry tree.

She was in a private hospital room.

"About time you woke up," stated a young nurse sitting next to the bed. She was prettier than her demeanor would suggest.

"Where am I?"

"A hospital in Tokyo. It's May first. You've been asleep almost two and a half days now, ever since that unidentified ambulance brought you in. You're bruised and sprained, but nothing's broken. If they gave you only one dose of those drugs—"

"Wait, who are you?"

"Ha ha. I guess I *don't* look like a nurse, after all. This uniform makes my shoulders stiff. If Sousuke weren't so rough, I wouldn't have to do these kinds of things."

"Sousuke? Are you one of his colleagues?"

"More or less . . . So, now that you're awake, I'll give you some advice: The bad guys at the base gave you drugs, and then you passed out. The next time you woke up, you were here, and you don't remember anything else. Forget about Sousuke, Kurz, the white AS, all that stuff."

"In other words, you want me to keep Mithril a secret?"

"Well, that's up to you. People connected with the Japanese military have heard of us. But if we—or you, yourself—were identified, the police probably wouldn't let you go home. So, keeping that in mind: You remember nothing. Stick to that story. I'm sure the police will question you tomorrow."

The faux nurse stood up. "Also, I want to thank you."

"Thank me?"

"Yes, Miss Chidori. You saved my men. They owe you their lives."

When the woman offered a handshake and a serious expression, Kaname found herself flustered.

"I, I didn't really—"

"I heard the story from Kurz. If you hadn't been there, he and Sousuke wouldn't have made it. Perhaps you're a stronger person than any of us."

"No way. This is embarrassing." Kaname laughed nervously.

Timidly, Kaname grasped the woman's slender fingers, which were alarmingly forceful.

"Well, I'll be going now."

"Um . . ."

"Yes?"

"What about Sagara?"

"Sousuke's already been assigned a new mission."

"Did he send a message?"

"To you? No, not specifically."

"Oh."

"Goodbye, then," the woman said as she left.

It was still raining outside.

Was Sousuke's mission already underway?

Was he out there, shivering in the rain? He could be in danger. He could be hurt.

Maybe someday, like a stray dog . . .

He could've had the courtesy to say goodbye, thought Kaname, her eyes starting to moisten. She wiped the tears with her sheets and buried her face in the pillow.

Five minutes later, a real doctor and nurse came by and informed Kaname that she was in very good shape. She would be able to leave as early as the next day. They also informed her that her father came to visit her, but he had returned to New York to work after he found out she would be fine.

After they left, another five minutes passed before a mob of students from Jindai High School filed in. There were all kinds of kids from class, the girls' softball team, and student council, as well as the principal, the vice-principal, Miss Kagurazaka, and of course, Kyouko.

"Kana!" Kyouko dove in full-speed for a high-impact hug.

Everyone crowded around, thrilled that Kaname was okay. They barraged her with their recounts of the events.

"We really were worried about you!"

"They let us off those planes at Fukuoka Airport."

"That rescue team totally just bailed, like they weren't part of the U.N. or anything!"

"It sounds like a conspiracy!"

"We didn't even know who to ask about you, Kana, and nobody knew . . ." Kyouko began.

"I'm so sorry, Chidori. I wish they'd taken me, instead. Maybe I'm not cut out to be a teacher."

"Oh, Kana!" sobbed Kyouko.

The merciless mob of well-wishers gave Kaname a real sense of being loved. It felt good to be home—really good.

"Hey, take it easy, guys," barked Kaname, unable to handle the commotion. "I'm still in the hospital, you know!"

"She's right," agreed one of the kids. "Even though the injuries are minor, she needs to rest."

Nodding, Kaname said, "That's right. Be careful with me! It looks like I'll get out of here tomorrow, though."

"Thanks to that rescue squad!"

"Yeah. It's a shame the class trip got ruined."

"Survival is the top priority."

"Right, survival is the . . ." Kaname trailed off, attempting to see who had said that. There, behind the weeping Miss Kagurazaka, stood a solitary male student with a sour face and tight lips under the shadow of his messy, black hair.

"S-Sagara?"

Everyone turned to Sousuke, wondering what was so special about *him.*

"Yes, Chidori?"

"What are you . . . um, why are you here?"

"How rude! I've come to see you and I also brought this." He thrust a pack full of treats in front of her.

"What the heck is this?"

"I'm the insurance policy," he mumbled.

"Insurance policy?"

"For the time being, at least."

"Oh, *great.*" Although she didn't say "thanks," the feigned irritation in Kaname's voice was entirely pleasant.

She took a deep breath and said, "You know, Sousuke, I've got some problems to discuss with you!"

And as Kaname started to air her grievances all at once, Sousuke panicked, frantically looking around for help.

Outside, it looked as though the rain would stop by nighttime.

AFTERWORD

This story is set in the present, but in a world with a more questionable outlook. Sousuke Sagara, who is part of Mithril (the world's mightiest high-tech mercenary force), accepts a new mission: to infiltrate a Tokyo high school and guard a certain girl. However, Sergeant Sagara has spent his life on the battlefield since he was young, so peaceful Japan is mostly a mystery to him. After a series of fruitless, berserk episodes, the high school girl he's supposed to protect ends up hating him.

That's how *Full Metal Panic!* begins.

If I had to put this story into a genre, it would be difficult. Its pages are a real melting pot. It would not be reasonable to call it a high school romantic comedy nor to label it a robot thing, and it isn't serious enough to be a military thriller. If I were forced to choose, perhaps I would call it an action adventure. I intended it to be seen as an action B movie, so please enjoy it at your own pace.

By the way, currently, in August of 1998, *Dragon Magazine* publishes the FMP short stories. These are utter campus comedies, set after the events in this book. They are laidback, slapstick stories that fully exhibit Sousuke's many acts of spaciness that cause Kaname to worry. In other words, they are more about everyday life. Thanks to your responses to the DM surveys, they seem pretty popular. For those who have not read them, I highly recommend that you do.

Of course, those of you who already are into the short stories might be surprised by the hard developments in this novel. I would be happy to know if you ever thought: "Sousuke's not an idiot, he's awesome!"

While I'm at it, I would like to comment on a few things.

1) The author harbors no ill will against a certain country that is integral to the plot. I was limited to choosing a dictatorship reachable by domestic flight. So, to those from that country, please do not abduct me. On the other hand, if I disappear or die in an accident—or if there's a mysterious fire at Fujimi Books—you readers know where to start the investigation.

2) At times, the story necessitates artifices intentionally be added to existing weapons, machines, organizations, and geography. Also, for all the common weapons introduced in the story, please

assume they have been more or less influenced by AS core technology. I'd be put to shame if I actually had to give specs.

3) At times, the story necessitates artifices intentionally be added to the mentality and private lives of actual girls. The high school girls in this story are more or less influenced by romantic-comedy core technology. I'd be put to shame if you took me seriously.

Now, I plan for Sousuke and crew to face many more troubles—don't worry, they'll probably get through it all, they'll just be out of breath. They are, after all, tough and tenacious.

That said, look forward to the future exploits of Sousuke and Kaname.

This marks the end of my tedious comments and the beginning of the part where I offer thanks:

To Takuzou Suganuma, editor-in-chief at *Dragon Magazine*, for funky advice and soulful cultivation of the story;

To Kazuma Shinjou, the novelist who had groovy advice and powerful resources;

To Tomoyuki Sano, the manga artist who provided cool images and dope ideas;

To Katou, Koyama, Watanabe, and Second Lieutenant Y.A., who offered beneficial data;

To all of you involved with the Chuo University SF club, which was the impetus for me choosing this line of work;

To Takahara Masaki; I offer a deep apology along with my thanks— I never thought ** would ** this far. I really am sorry. Someday, ** will **;

To Shikidouji, who, despite other work pressures, fitted the book with charming illustrations;

To Kumiko Satou, the editor who helped me finally complete the book;

And to Cassie: If this young girl hadn't spilled chocolate milk all over the manuscript, the ending might have been totally different (kidding).

Well, I'll see you next time when, once again, Sousuke flirts with hell.

— Shoji Gatoh, August 1998